Digital Marketing
IN THE **ZONE**

Digital
Marketing
IN THE
ZONE

The Ultimate System for
Digital Marketing Success

DAVID RESKE

NEW YORK

NASHVILLE • MELBOURNE • VANCOUVER

Digital Marketing IN THE ZONE
The Ultimate System for Digital Marketing Success

Published in New York, New York, by Morgan James Publishing. Morgan James is a trademark of Morgan James, LLC. www.MorganJamesPublishing.com

The Morgan James Speakers Group can bring authors to your live event. For more information or to book an event visit The Morgan James Speakers Group at www.TheMorganJamesSpeakersGroup.com.

ISBN 978-1-68350-268-5 paperback
ISBN 978-1-68350-269-2 eBook
Library of Congress Control Number: 2016916258

Cover Design by:
Chris Treccani
www.3dogdesign.net

Interior Design by:
Bonnie Bushman
The Whole Caboodle Graphic Design

In an effort to support local communities, raise awareness and funds, Morgan James Publishing donates a percentage of all book sales for the life of each book to Habitat for Humanity Peninsula and Greater Williamsburg.

Get involved today! Visit
www.MorganJamesBuilds.com

Table of Contents

Preface
My Journey into the Zone

I started my first company in 1994 with the simple idea that people should be able to use their PCs to access a database of computer products online where they could search and compare products, and then make a purchase. These were the days of dial-up modems before Internet Explorer and Netscape Navigator, and no one knew then how important the Internet would be in all of our lives. I was in the MBA program at Boston University at the time, and after I wrote the business plan, I got so excited that I quit my job selling computers, quit the MBA program and started Online Computer Market, Inc. With two kids under age three at home, I suddenly had no income and a lot of pressure to get the business off the ground.

As a young entrepreneur, I didn't know much about technology or building a business, but I knew how to sell, so the first thing I did was call on computer companies to get my first customer. It was tough and I spent months making phone calls and doing presentations, and hit a lot of brick walls. There were many nights I'd stay awake scared that we'd lose our house, or worse. My wife Trish and I got very good at spending very little money on food and everyday expenses, and every day I woke up more determined than ever to make the business work.

After a lot of conversations with computer companies, I slowly realized that no one wanted to put their products online where they could be easily "shopped" against their competitors — at least not in 1994. Unfortunately, my original business plan was a few years too early.

Fortunately, I realized that what they all really wanted was a website.

Although I didn't know it at the time, 1994 turned out to be the beginning of the commercialization of the Internet, and soon everyone wanted to get on the web. I quickly pivoted the business and started building websites while hiring people as fast as possible. It was an exciting time, and I learned a lot about building a company. I made many mistakes in those early years, but because we had a strong demand for our services, we survived and grew rapidly.

By 1998 we had 50 people on staff and a lot of debt, so after a lot of soul searching, I decided to sell the company to a large professional services organization that promised to take care of the employees and continue to grow the business. I stayed on for a couple of years to help with the transition, but then it was time to do something new.

In 2003, I started another business, Nowspeed, Inc., which focused exclusively on digital marketing. My goal was not to grow large and fast like my first business, but simply to do excellent digital marketing and work with a small team who could make a big impact for our clients. We started with email marketing, and then added Google PPC and SEO services the following year. Soon we were building websites and landing pages too. In 2007, we added social media marketing services and then marketing automation services as marketing technology evolved. Every time a new innovation or marketing technology came along, we spent a lot of time learning how to use it to drive strong, consistent and predictable results. Not all of our campaigns were successful, but we worked extremely hard to make them work and deliver good results for our clients.

Today we still build websites, but we also provide deep Inbound and Content Marketing services using the best SEO, Digital Advertising, Social Media, Marketing Automation and Email marketing tools and techniques available. Over the past 13+ years, I've personally worked with hundreds of clients from the very small to the very large, and learned a lot about digital marketing systems and people along the way.

I wrote this book because I've met many, many wonderful people through my client relationships over the years who were all trying hard to be successful in their marketing campaigns and do a good job. Time after time, however, I saw people who were working very hard make bad choices using flawed strategies that produced poor results. Once these companies hired us and we started to apply the strategies I will share in this book, they often moved to a happy and confident place I call the Zone.

It's been an amazing ride to watch the industry evolve over the last 20 years. My goal is to share my experience in this book to help you move into the Zone so that you can be successful and confident in your digital marketing efforts. When you get there, I hope you will share your experience with me and others, so that we make the Zone a big, happy and successful place.

Acknowledgments

I'm grateful to so many people who've supported me in writing this book. My wife, Trish, who co-founded Nowspeed with me, was always there to support me in building our businesses, while taking care of our four children and giving me the time I needed to write. She is a wonderful writer herself, and always inspired me and encouraged me to finish, even when I couldn't see the light at the end of the writing tunnel.

I'm also grateful to the team at Nowspeed who worked with me to develop the strategies that help our clients move into the Zone every day. I'm especially grateful for the input from Tom McGovern, Jillian Wallace and Justin Stanley who lead our work with clients every day. Along with many other current and former Nowspeed team members, they helped me develop the methodologies presented in this book and prove it out time after time in real client engagements. I'm also grateful for the time they took to read and provide feedback on key chapters of this book.

I'm grateful to my clients for teaching me as much about business and life as I taught them about marketing. I've worked with so many wonderful people over the years, and am constantly awed by the trust they've placed in me and our team to produce good results week after week. I've included many of their stories in this book, but have changed the names of the people and companies to maintain confidentiality.

I'm also grateful to the people who took the time to read the manuscript and give me important feedback and ideas. I want to first thank my copy editor, Jessica Filippi, who was extremely helpful in providing detailed edits to move the project forward. I'm especially grateful for the detailed feedback from Joel Goldstein, Zara Al-Harazi, Bill Flynn, Carol Slicklen and Evan Zall. I'm blown away that they took the time to read my rough draft and give me thoughtful and detailed feedback.

Lastly, I'm grateful to my parents, Arnold and Ella Reske, who are always such an inspiration for me through their faith and positive attitude toward life. They have always loved and believed in me to do so much more than I thought possible. They lead a simple life and are loved by many, and it reminds me that I don't need money or stuff to be successful in life.

Digital Marketing
in the Zone

I
n this age of marketing complexity, some marketers have risen above the fray and are accelerating the results of their digital marketing campaigns. They have a complete view of the market and their place in it, and have strategies and plans that work. They are not confused at all about the types of campaigns that are available, and they have complete confidence in the ads, messages, offers, and content they are producing.

In my experience with hundreds of clients over the past 20 years, I've observed that most marketers don't live life this way. Instead, they struggle with their campaigns and live in a perpetual state of confusion, wishful thinking, and risk-taking. Along with their professional frustrations, they experience negative emotions and are never totally happy with their work.

Some marketers, however, move into a Zone where they are confident and successful in their programs, and can rest knowing that their campaigns will work time and time again. They

1

experience satisfaction and even joy as they do good work and drive strong results.

Marketing has changed dramatically in the past 20 years, and many marketers are struggling to keep up. When marketers had few metrics and little accountability, it was easy to be confident. Often the biggest challenge was developing ad creative and content that your boss liked. Once the campaigns were launched, it was so difficult to measure success that any result was fine and the pressure was off. The best marketers were good at creative design, messaging, and managing campaign budgets. Performance and results were not that important because no one knew exactly how to measure success.

Today, most marketing programs are measurable, and marketers are under increasing pressure to produce results. Marketers increasingly feel that they are on quota and are accountable for a sophisticated set of metrics and key performance indicators every week. There is a lot of pressure when the expected results don't materialize and management wants to know why.

In addition to the new culture of accountability, marketers today have a lot more campaign complexity. In the past, they could rely on their agency partners to produce and manage radio, print, and TV ads; produce collateral; and manage trade shows. These channels are still important, but marketers today must also have a detailed understanding of search and email marketing, SEO, marketing software, and website analytics.

Successful marketers today are completely comfortable with the latest marketing techniques and technologies in search, mobile, social media, and website design, and are excited about leveraging new marketing techniques before their competitors are even aware of them. They are living in the Zone.

Not every campaign goes well for these marketers, but they constantly make small bets and have a clear understanding of what needs to be tested and how to use the test results.

My goal for you is to be one of these marketers. This book will help you understand the world of digital marketing strategies, tools, and techniques and enable you to move away from frustrating guesswork so that your campaigns deliver solid results.

Once you start implementing the principles in this book, you'll be happier and less stressed about your marketing campaigns, and your career will move faster and with less effort.

Six Core Elements:
Marketing in the Zone

M arketing in the Zone is a system of six core elements that you must master in order to be a world-class marketer. You can master these strategies and be more confident and successful no matter how large your company is, or how many team members you have. They apply to any industry in any country.

The first step is to have a clear understanding of your marketing strategy. With digital marketing it's tempting to dive right in and build a new website, or a launch a Google Adwords campaign, but you need to have a solid strategy in place first, before any of those programs have a chance of success. As a prerequisite, you need to get a clear understanding of your customers, competitors, and channel partners, as well as your past digital marketing campaigns. This foundation is critical for every aspect of your work. In order to build your strategy, you'll also need to get clarity on the mission of your organization and set clear marketing goals that are aligned with the overall goals of your organization.

4

Once you have these elements in place, you can move to building personas in order to get a clear understanding of your target audience, and creating differentiated messaging to set you apart. This strategic process will let you create a plan and budget that's completely in alignment with your strategy.

The second step is to develop the people and processes needed to achieve your goals. People are critical to effective marketing, and you'll need to spend a lot of time and energy to build the right team. I'll show you how to find the right people, make sure they are in the right roles, and regularly evaluate them to make sure you've got the team you need. Your team will probably also include outside service providers, so I'll show you how to select and evaluate them, too. Once you have the right team members in place, you'll need to create an organizational cadence that gets things done and create effective meetings to keep everything on track.

The third element is data and technology, since digital marketing is impossible without software and the Internet. By selecting the right technology and using it effectively, you can make a big impact quickly. Today there are literally thousands of marketing applications available, so it's important to have a process to select and continuously evaluate your vendor partners to make sure you have the tools you need. I'll show you how to build marketing technology architecture for your organization that will let you quickly identify and master the right software. In this section, I'll also show you how to get the data you need to make good decisions.

Once you have a solid strategy, the right people, and a good set of technological tools in place, you'll be ready to start working on your marketing content, website, and programs. Strong content is a critical component of any digital marketing program, and I'll show you how to create a content plan that's in sync with what your buyers need throughout the buying cycle. From there, I'll show you how to create a plan for a website that will make a big impact on your business, build your brand, and showcase your content.

The last element in the Zone is your marketing programs themselves. Here's where I'll get specific and show you how build and manage the campaigns that will drive strong results. I'll give you specific ways you can improve your email, advertising, social media, and other marketing programs to get more for less. At the end of this section, I'll also show you how to create test programs in order to optimize each element and continually improve your results.

You'll notice from the image above that the Zone process is a circle, so once you've finished the cycle once, you'll be ready to revisit your strategy, process, and technology choices based on what you've learned. This system will keep you on track and make you successful and confident for years to come.

Zone Marketing Checkup

Self-assessment is an important first step to move forward into the Zone. Rate yourself on the following statements, where 1 is weak and 5 is very strong.

Are you in the Zone?	1	2	3	4	5
1. We have a clear marketing strategy that is completely in sync with the organizational mission and vision.					
2. We have specific, documented marketing goals that are aligned with our organization's sales goals.					
3. Our executive leadership fully understands and supports our marketing plan.					
4. We have a weekly scorecard in place for each marketing area that provides a clear view of our progress against our goals.					
5. We have a marketing plan in place and it clearly shows how our marketing investments will enable us to reach our goals.					
6. We have a strong understanding of our customers' and/or channel partners' key purchase criteria and needs.					
7. We have a strong understanding of our competitors and we keep up to date monthly with all of their activities, strategies, and marketing programs.					
8. We have clearly defined marketing personas with strong, differentiated messaging to reach each persona.					
9. Everyone on the team understands the marketing mission, vision, and plan.					
10. Everyone on the marketing team knows how their work impacts the plan, and has clear metrics to focus on each week.					

11. We have excellent and productive weekly and quarterly meetings that enable us to plan, track progress, and deal with issues.					
12. We have the right people on the marketing team and we regularly assess the quality of our in-house team.					
13. All of our team members are well trained, certified, follow our processes, and drive innovation.					
14. All of our service providers are excellent and deliver strong value.					
15. We have documented processes in place for all of the core marketing functions.					
16. We have all of the content necessary to meet the needs of each market segment across all phases of the buying process, buying cycle, or customer journey.					
17. We have a documented marketing technology architecture that includes all of the software tools we need to be effective.					
18. We regularly evaluate the quality and fit of each element of our marketing technology.					
19. We are testing content, messages, advertising, and marketing channels each month and we make regular changes based on what we learn.					
20. All of our marketing programs are producing results according to plan.					
21. Our marketing budget is sufficient to enable us achieve our goals.					
22. Our website fully reflects our brand and key messages with excellent design and strong content.					

23. Our website does a good job of getting traffic through SEO and converting visitors to leads or sales.					
24. Our digital advertising programs are efficient and effective, producing leads and sales at or below industry cost averages.					
25. Our social media campaigns are growing followers faster than our competitors, and are driving strong engagement, traffic, leads, and sales.					
26. We are effective at reaching out to all influencers including bloggers, analysts, and press.					
27. We have a large email house list that includes most of the buyers in our target market.					
28. Our email program is effective and drives strong results with every email blast.					
29. Our marketing automation system is fully implemented across all market segments and each phase of the buying cycle.					
30. We have a plan to innovate in every area of our marketing programs mix each quarter.					
Total					

Zone Checkup Results

If you scored between 10 and 40%, this book is for you. You've got a lot of challenges ahead and need a path to get there. If you scored between 41 and 60%, you're average with room for improvement. If you scored above 60%, you're above average and you should find a few ideas here to take you all the way into the Zone.

The Beginnings of Measurable Marketing

Marketers have tried for years to create ways to track the effectiveness of their campaigns so that they could be confident of consistent results. In the 1930s, Arthur Nielsen created a rating system for radio campaigns that he later expanded to television in the 1950s. This system began with user diaries where people in different demographic target markets recorded what they listened to and watched. Later it evolved to automated set meters, which were more accurate, but still relied on statistical projections to determine what people were watching.

The Nielsen system told television and radio advertisers roughly how many people were watching their ads, in about the same way that newspapers or magazines tell advertisers how many people are seeing their ads. A newspaper may print and distribute 100,000 copies, but they have no way of knowing how many people actually see the ad inside the paper.

Billboard and event advertisers also have this problem. If you buy a billboard where 50,000 cars, buses, and trucks per week pass the sign, you have no way of knowing how many people actually read it.

Since marketers could only get inaccurate and incomplete data from their radio, TV, newspaper, billboard, or other traditional advertising, they could only roughly correlate their advertising spending with store traffic, phone calls, or sales.

It was even more difficult for small advertisers. If you were trying to advertise a restaurant, a retail store, or a small consulting or service business, your options in the past were limited to the Yellow Pages, direct mail or newspaper ads, and it was often impossible to connect your marketing investments directly to business results.

Yes, the Yellow Pages ad might have made the phone ring, but did it ring enough to pay for the ad and create a positive return on investment? Most small advertisers gave up even trying to answer these questions accurately and simply paid the monthly Yellow Pages bill.

Digital Marketing Trends

Digital Marketing brought the ability to target and track advertising much more easily than traditional marketing, but it has changed dramatically in the past 20 years since the beginning of the commercial use of the Internet when websites and email marketing dominated the landscape. During the first 10 years of the commercialization of the Internet, from 1994 to 2004, marketers were able to create websites as online brochures and drive traffic to their websites using email.

Email proved to be a very effective tool, but it annoyed many users and unwanted commercial messages earned the label "spam." The goal of many online campaigns became to capture email addresses so that you could market to them later by email. Marketers also purchased email lists and spammed millions of people. Spam became so bad that the US government stepped in and created the CAN SPAM[1] act to control the way messages were sent and give users to the ability to opt out of commercial email messages. Other governments followed and created even more restrictive email laws.

High-quality advertisers quickly adapted to this regulation, so it had a limited impact on most companies' marketing programs. The larger impact came from Internet Service Providers and email software vendors, such as Microsoft and Google, who filtered out spam email before users could see it. The result of these changes meant that the email response rates dropped significantly during this time, and email changed from a customer acquisition tool to a customer nurturing tool.

Banner ads on websites were also used for years, but they were not very effective. Ad networks sold banner ads the way people sold newspaper ads. You got visibility on a website with your banner ad, but the results were inconsistent and hard to track.

---

1   Source: CAN-SPAM_Act_of_2003. Footnote at www.marketing-in-the-zone.com/footnotes

In 2004, search marketing started to grow significantly as an efficient way to drive traffic and get results. Google offered the ability to advertise on keywords, but instead of paying by impression, you paid per click in a live auction system with other advertisers. Suddenly it became possible for thousands of new advertisers to drive traffic to their websites from a specific audience very cost-effectively. By bidding on a specific keyword and then offering an ad tailored to that particular search, you could drive traffic to specific landing pages and capture leads or increase sales.

Search Engine Optimization also grew rapidly during this time since marketers also wanted to take advantage of free traffic from the search engines. Search Engine Optimization (SEO) is the art and science of turning your website into what the search engines want to see, so that you appear higher in the natural (free) search engine rankings and you get more traffic to your website.

Search marketing and display advertising are the largest parts of most digital marketing budgets today. Search marketing is forecast to grow from $35 billion in 2016 to $45 billion in 2019[2]. Display advertising is almost as big, growing from $28 billion to $37 billion during the same period of time[3].

In 2007, social media changed the landscape again for digital marketers. Websites such as Facebook, LinkedIn, and Twitter gave people the ability to interact directly and share their experiences with each other online outside of the control of advertisers. Marketers no longer controlled the conversation; they had to learn to participate in the conversation and gain influence with their customers. With the growth of social media usage came social media advertising. Social media advertising is growing from $11 billion in US spending in 2016 to $17 billion by 2019[4].

2   Source: Forrester Research. Footnote at www.marketing-in-the-zone.com/
      footnotes
3   IBID
4   IBID

Another recent major trend is the growth in mobile advertising. Since the launch of the iPhone in 2007, people worldwide have adopted smartphones as a way to communicate with each other and connect to the Internet. Mobile advertising grew to $42 billion in ad revenue in 2016, and is projected to grow to $65 billion by 2019[5]. This massive growth rate reflects the fact that people are spending more of their time on mobile devices and less on traditional PCs.

These changes mark a radical shift in the advertising landscape that was dominated by radio, TV, and print advertising only a few short years ago, and demonstrate that advertisers are increasingly confident that they are getting solid returns from Digital Marketing.

Paid Digital Advertising and Earned Media

Digital advertising makes it much easier to connect the dots between marketing investments and business results. With paid digital ads, you can create online ads that are displayed on search engines and websites across the Internet, and then track the clicks from your ads to specific pages on your website. When people buy a product or register as a lead, you can see exactly which ads produced the result. This takes the guesswork out of marketing and advertising. You know which ads are working and which are not working, so you can finally see where your advertising is being wasted—and do something about it.

Online marketing today, however, is so much broader than paid advertising. A website is now essentially a business storefront or an extra sales team member selling goods and services. Anyone who visits the website is a potential customer, and there are many ways you can drive traffic without paying for it directly. For example, you can get listed in directories, mentioned on other people's blogs, or syndicate content through social media sites such as Twitter, LinkedIn, and Facebook.

---

5   Source: Emarketer. Footnote at www.marketing-in-the-zone.com/footnotes

All of these activities can produce traffic to your website that you don't have to pay for directly. It does, however, take time and effort to create and manage the distribution of the content required to produce results. Because of this, you should assign a cost to these efforts, just as you track the cost of paid online advertising, and then track the results against the cost to create a return on investment calculation for each type of marketing activity.

Trackable vs. Non Trackable Activity— Branding vs. Direct Response

While a lot of digital marketing activity is trackable, there is still a lot that we don't know about how ads influence behavior. For example, I recently met with a B2B client where year-to-date we produced 18 million ad impressions, 52,253 clicks to their website, and 3,836 leads. This company can tell exactly what happened to these leads by tracking their sales activity through their CRM (customer relationship management system), but they don't know the influence that the 18 million ad impressions had on other behavior.

Will the ad impression make people more likely to respond to a sales call or another ad in the future? Will they cause people to recommend the product to a colleague? We don't know the answers to these questions, so advertisers often chalk this type of marketing activity up to "branding."

Since this type of visibility might be helpful at some future time, companies are often tempted to set up a branding budget and just get visibility for their company. This type of thinking can lead to bad marketing investments because you are deliberately spending money on media that cannot be tracked. It's better to get branding as a byproduct of direct response marketing than the other way around.

If this client wanted to just get ad impressions, they could have spent the money and not tracked the results. But by focusing on clicks and leads, they got both brand visibility and leads. If you just focus on brand visibility, that's all you get—and you can't track it. Does this mean that the brand visibility has no value? Of course not; but because it's not trackable, it should not be the main goal of your campaign.

Strategies to Accelerate Your Results

In order to accelerate your marketing results, you'll need to connect the dots between all of your marketing activities so that you can quickly and easily see what works, and then make rapid adjustments to continuously improve your results. To do this you'll need to blend the creative right-brain side of marketing with a left-brain analytical approach to get the best results.

Although you should always be testing new ideas, you should spend more and more of your marketing budget on proven techniques, media and messages that produce results. The testing will create a continuous improvement cycle that will allow you to produce better and better outcomes.

In order to track and optimize your campaigns, you'll need to develop a solid understanding of how a prospect moves through the buying process. In a B2B sale, they may start as a "click" and then turn into a lead, a qualified lead, a proposal, and then finally a customer over many months or years. In a B2C e-commerce business, that process may happen in a matter of moments. Whatever business you are in, it's critical to set up an integrated tracking process so that you understand how your marketing investments drive results at every stage of the buying process.

To accelerate your digital marketing program, you'll need to use the most effective online marketing tools. Paid Search, Digital Advertising, Organic Search (SEO), Website, Email, Social Media, Video, and Mobile marketing tools have evolved to be highly targeted, allowing you to drive effective results. These techniques all have different characteristics, but can be used together or separately to drive leads or increase sales. They are also highly trackable so that you can understand the outcomes of your spending.

Many direct marketers have been using these strategies for years in direct mail campaigns. Since direct mail is expensive to produce, the conventional approach is to always test at least two messages against each other until you find the best one that works consistently. Volume mailers will test the message on the outside of the envelope, the format of the letter, the headline, the body copy, the call to action, and even the signature. Testing at this level is expensive and requires dozens of mailings large enough to be statistically significant.

To create a test plan for a direct mail campaign, you'd start by developing a test hypothesis. That is, you'd develop two creative ideas that you believe will both be successful and test them against each other. Then you send at least 5,000 direct mail pieces to different segments of the same list and test for the response rate. If test group A beats test group B, you can then continue to develop new creatives and test them against the winner in order to produce new results.

Although this process is effective, it can be expensive and is used consistently by only the largest direct mail companies. Internet marketing makes this testing process much less expensive, faster, and more efficient, and you can use it to improve every aspect of your Internet marketing program. It can also be used by marketers of every size, from the largest Fortune 500 company to the smallest retail business.

In an email campaign, for example, it's much less expensive to create and test two subject lines against each other, then test two headlines, offers, and calls to action. In just a few rounds of testing with a few thousand emails, you can quickly find the most effective subject line, headline, offer, and key message. You can also find out which list or segment of your list is most effective.

You can also use this testing process to make your website produce more leads. If your website is not effective, the traditional approach would be to throw out the entire website and create a new site that you hope is better. If you go this route, you'll be able to compare the lead conversion rate of the site before and after the change, but you won't know specifically what caused the change in the first place.

A better approach would be to test different website elements against each other; for example, you may start by featuring different offers to see which works best. If you are a B2C marketer, you may try featuring different catalog items on the home page to see which improves sales the most. A B2B marketer can feature different white papers or consultation offers on the home page to see which is most effective.

This process of testing and continuous improvement can be used at every level until you run out of offers, messages, or ideas to test. The important thing is to be creative and then test your ideas scientifically to learn how the marketplace responds.

By adopting a methodical approach to marketing, you'll be using the best online marketing tools available, connecting the dots between your investments and results, and tracking customer responses all the way through the buying process.

Get in the Zone

Digital Marketing in the Zone is a system for creating a digital marketing program that drives results for your business with perfect confidence that it will be successful. You will not only build a strong strategy, but you will also develop marketing programs that create the best marketing results for your organization and continuously improve those results over time.

To get into the Zone, you'll need to understand your customers and competitors, and then use that understanding to create a new marketing strategy for your company. You'll also need to leverage the best digital marketing tools and techniques, as well as how to leverage data to learn from and improve your campaigns.

I hope that by using the principles and techniques in this book, you will achieve more success and professional happiness than you ever dreamed of.

Additional Resources

Visit www.marketing-in-the-zone.com for additional resources.

- **Zone Marketing Checkup**. This self-assessment is an important first step to move forward into the Zone.

Part I

Accelerating Your Marketing Strategy

Strategy in the Zone

I f you don't know where you are going, you're going to feel lost. No matter how well your campaigns seem to be working, you may have this nagging feeling that you're headed in the wrong direction. And even if you seem to be successful, you won't be happy about it.

On the other hand, once you know where you are going, even minor setbacks can't keep you from achieving your goals, and you'll be able to be totally happy and confident in your success.

With the right strategy, you'll be ready to create plans and programs that will let you win, and—more importantly—you'll know why you're winning.

In order to accelerate your marketing programs, you need to have a solid marketing strategy in place and use it as the foundation of all of your campaigns. It's critical to know who your target customers are, what's most important to them, and how you compare to your competitors on these dimensions. This understanding will lead you to your positioning and enable you to create differentiated messages that will drive all of your marketing.

If you get this right, you'll be hitting the bull's-eye with every message every time. If you get this wrong, you'll be spending your money on the wrong messages sent to the wrong people. You can test your way to the right messages over time, but it will be much easier and less expensive if you start in the right direction.

Once you have this foundation in place, you can create a detailed marketing plan that will start with benchmark metrics in all the important areas of digital marketing, and then plan for improvements over time. This plan will be the basis for all of your future marketing activities, so it's worth taking the time to build a solid plan.

Situation Analysis: How are you doing now?			
Customers	Competitors	Partners	Current Programs

Objectives: What are your goals and how do you measure success?	
Mission and Vision	Goals, KPIs and Analytics

Strategy: How can you achieve your goals?			
Personas	Differentiation	Messaging/Stories	Budget & Calendar

Situation Analysis

Customers

Before you can create a marketing strategy, you need to know where you are starting. If you have an existing business, the best place to start is to talk to your current customers. You can learn a lot by asking simple questions about who they are, what they want, and why they bought products or services from you instead of your competitors. You can also ask them what they like or don't like about your company and any suggestions they have for improvements. If your business sells through a channel of distribution, you can also talk to your channel partners to fully understand their needs and wants.

At my agency, we call every client every quarter with a short survey, and review what we learn in our weekly Operations meeting. We also rate the happiness of every client every week. By doing this, we are working hard to fully understand their needs and keep our services in sync with our market.

Competitive Intelligence

While you are building your marketing strategy and marketing plan, it's also important to understand what your competitors are doing. You may want to copy them or do the exact opposite, but it's extremely important to be fully informed about what they are up to. Fortunately, the web has made it much easier to get a good understanding of your competitors.

To get started, go online with the following checklist:

Website and Messaging:
- What does their core messaging say about how they believe they are different?
- Who are their best customers?
- Is their website well designed?
- Is it easy to find content on their website?
- Does it clearly communicate what their products and services do and why they are different?
- Is it clear what market segments they serve and what is compelling for each one?
- Does it strategically lead the user to compelling offers?
- Are their landing pages effectively designed?

- How well have they integrated social media into their website?
- How well is it optimized for organic search?
- Advertising and Search: Search on the most important keywords for your industry.
- How visible are they on the most important keywords for organic search?
- Are they advertising on paid search?
- Are their ads compelling and do they lead to well-designed landing pages?
- Are the offers on their landing pages compelling?
- Are the tags on their website optimized for specific keywords?
- Are they advertising across other websites?
- Email: Sign up for their email newsletter or register on their website.
- Are their emails professional and well designed?
- Do their emails feature strong offers?
- Do they automatically deliver nurturing emails designed to drive users through the buying cycle?

Social Media and Content:
- How many followers do they have on each of the major social media sites?
- How much content are they posting to each of the sites each week?
- How interactive are they with their audience?
- How many of their posts are about their company and products vs. thought leadership content?
- Do they have a compelling blog with solid content?

Your competitor's web site will tell you a tremendous amount about their marketing strategy and messaging. Once you get the data on each of these items, evaluate the answers against other content and best practices listed in this book to build a full view on each competitor.

Current Programs

Before you start creating any new strategies or marketing programs, it's important to learn from the past in order to understand which strategies and tactics have been successful and which have been unsuccessful. Some organizations are good at documenting organizational marketing learning, but most are not. As you assemble the experiences of the past, you should create a library of findings in one place, so you can avoid reinventing the wheel.

During the process of reviewing existing campaigns, you'll learn clues about where to start with your new marketing campaigns. For example, if paid search advertising has worked well in the past, that may be a key element of your new campaign strategy. If it has not worked well, you may need to dig a little deeper to find out why. I always like to find out if a certain campaign can't work for a particular company or industry, or if it didn't work because it was simply executed badly.

Once you have a good understanding of your customers, competitors, channel partners and campaigns, you'll be ready to start setting objectives.

Objectives

Setting objectives can be a very challenging task. If you set your goals too high, you'll run the risk of failure. You may dramatically improve your results, but not hit the lofty goals you set. If you set your goals too low, you may be accused of sandbagging.

Before you can set your marketing objectives, you must understand the mission and vision of your organization. Is your organization all about brand impact, social impact, sales growth, online sales, or customer engagement? Each of these organizational goals will drive a different type of marketing campaign and marketing mix. For example, if your organization's marketing goal is to build a world-class brand, you may focus on ad strategies and content that deliver high-impact messages to a wide audience and measure your impact by the number of ad impressions. If your organization is focused on growing sales, you may want to put all of your effort behind driving qualified sales leads.

Once you have a good understanding of the goals of your company, you'll need to translate them into specific marketing goals, Key Performance Indicators (KPIs), and set up the analytics necessary to track the results. This is a challenging process, but the planning methods described later in this chapter should help you get there.

Strategy

Personas: Your best customer profile

When you build a marketing plan, you need to know who to focus on. Ready, Fire, Aim is not a strategy that will drive results for marketers any more than it drives results for marksmen.

To build an effective view of your best target customers, you need to start by carefully understanding what makes your potential customers different from each other. This process is called market segmentation or persona building. If you are selling a product in a B2B market, your potential customers might need to be addressed differently because of their:

- Industry
- Location
- Role within the company
- Level within the company
- Size of the company
- Experience

If you are selling to a B2C market, you might need to address customers differently by:

- Age
- Sex
- Location
- Income Level
- Education
- Technical Skills
- Shopping Patterns

These are just starting sets of potential customer demographic differences. There are many more potential segmentation variables that you might consider based on your specific market.

Once you understand the segmentation variables, you'll need to decide how to break up your segments within each variable. If you are selling cars, you might address people differently if they are under 18, 19–35, 36–50, and over 50 years old. If you are selling LEGOs, your age segmentation might be under 6, 7–9, 10–12, 13–15, 16–18 and over 18 years old. The number of segments you create for each segmentation variable will determine how detailed a plan you'll need to build to address each market.

Align Your Marketing Campaigns with Your Personas

I thought that this was our most successful, longest running campaign—until I got the call. John had taken over as the VP of Marketing at a client company a few months earlier. He seemed impressed with our work and eager to keep us going since our consistent lead flow was substantial and our cost per lead was incredibly low.

This company sold software through channels such as VARs (Value Added Resellers) and passed the leads that we generated to their channel partners, so they never really knew if their leads turned into customers or not. Still, they wanted to keep sending the leads to their VARs because they believed that it built their relationship with their resellers and that many of the leads would ultimately become customers.

John called me because he was frustrated and ready to cancel the search marketing lead generation program. He did not see enough quality leads coming from the program, and didn't think we were focused on the right keywords or featuring the right landing pages or white papers as offers.

This was a little confusing, since we had met with his marketing manager and his PR manager each month and reviewed the keywords, offers and landing pages with them in great detail. We'd even received strong positive feedback on the number of raw leads that were turning into quality leads and being passed to their resellers.

John was frustrated because his team and our team were only focused on improving the core campaign metrics, and not on the real business results. Even though our lead flow and cost per lead were strong, he was not seeing the quality leads he wanted.

When I dug into the campaign and looked at the actual leads, I saw that many of them were from the Middle East, Afghanistan, and Pakistan. Even though they had authorized our campaigns in these regions, I knew that if most of our leads were from these areas, they would not be happy.

We met with John and his team and presented the data and our findings and recommended that we target the campaign on only countries he really was focused on. We also recommended that we remove all but the most relevant white papers from the campaign and change the landing page to ensure that all of the required fields had to be filled out.

Within days, the campaign started producing quality leads for his sales team. The cost per lead was higher than the old campaign, but there were many more quality leads and the client felt that the campaign was moving in the right direction. John signed on with Nowspeed for another year.

The important lesson here was that it's not enough to make the core campaign metrics move in the right direction. You need to understand the real business goals of the campaign and focus on them.

By aligning the client's strategy with our campaigns, John became much more confident and happy with the results. He moved from frustration to the Zone.

Buyer Personas

Once you have your segmentation variables in place, you're ready to create buyer personas. This step is where you get in touch with your customers in order to understand who they are, what they like, and how they buy.

First, consider your customers' goals, their characteristics, and their obstacles or challenges. When you think about their objectives, remember to consider both their personal and professional goals. What are their personal objectives? What do they really want to get out of this product or solution personally? What are their professional objectives? What business goals do they want to accomplish?

In terms of their personal characteristics, what's their title? Where are they located? What experience do they have? What are some trigger events that might be moving them to look for a solution to their problem?

Once you understand their goals and characteristics, you can start to understand the challenges they face. This step is where you put all of your research and analytics together and start to think about who your ideal customer is. When you create personas, it's best to give each one a name and actually create a picture of your ideal customer.

Here's an example of a persona: Chloe is a U.S.-based marketing director in the healthcare industry with 5 years' experience in digital advertising, but she's struggling with how to use mobile advertising effectively in order to achieve her company's marketing goals so that she can get a promotion.

In this example, you can see how we've included her objectives, characteristics, and obstacles in order to describe a persona that seems real. By using personas, you can be more specific about the kind of content that's going to be helpful, not just to the general market, but to Chloe, a person you can actually visualize. This will help you make your content and programs more tangible.

When you first start developing personas, start with no more than 3 to 5, so that you can focus on a few of the most important personas who are going to make a difference to your organization. By focusing on a few, you'll avoid getting bogged down and creating too many that you won't be able to adequately address. It will also be a much easier to develop great content for the most important personas rather than mediocre content or just a thin layer of content for all the personas you might imagine.

The Buyer's Journey

As you build your marketing plan, you will quickly realize that the content and programs you need for a buyer who is early in the buying process are very different than the content and programs you need for buyers who are about to make a purchase. If you want to create content that matters, you'll need to do so for your customers and prospects throughout the entire buyer's journey. In most complex purchasing decisions, buyers often go through an awareness phase, an evaluation phase, and a purchase phase.

To understand your buyer's journey, look at your own marketplace and ask yourself how your buyers make decisions. In every market and in every industry, this is going to be a little bit different. In general, buyers start their journey by identifying an issue or problem that they are having. Then they start researching potential solutions to the problem. From there, they start evaluating products and then potential vendors. Finally, they study alternative products and vendors so that they can make a decision. Along the way, they come up with a list of criteria that will help them make a decision.

Let me give you two examples of how this works in different situations. When high school students and their parents make a buying decision for college, they start by going through a process to try to figure out where they want to go to school and what they are interested in studying. Then they start reviewing and reading material from specific schools. They might also look at *U.S. News & World Report* or other publications that show college rankings. From there, they might look at potential schools in their area, talk to friends, and explore social media conversations. They may also look at school websites and talk to people at certain schools before they start narrowing down their list.

During this time, they will develop decision criteria that will help them sort out their options as they visit different schools. Finally, the student actually applies to a school or multiple schools, and then makes a decision once he or she is accepted. It's a very long, complicated process and the buyers consume a lot of information along the way.

Let's contrast this with a business-to-business example in a large company. If you're an IT buyer—let's say you're a director of IT—you might identify a problem where you don't have the right disaster recovery capabilities within your organization. To solve this problem, you will go through a very different process.

You start by fully understanding the problem: "What if there is a fire in my data center? What do I do?" Then you research solutions. You might look at what analysts are saying. You might read articles, blogs, and white papers. You might read examples of how other people solved this problem by asking questions on social media. In addition, you might also go to an event or conference to learn more.

While you are learning about options, studying alternatives, and talking to vendors, you will also be building a set of decision criteria to help you choose the best solution. Once you finish your research, you will start evaluating vendors and products and finally make a purchase decision.

These are just two examples, and for your industry there may be a totally different type of buying process. You must understand what your buyers are actually doing to make buying decisions in order to create appropriate content to communicate with them across the entire buying cycle.

From these two examples, I'm sure you can see the importance of engaging with your buyer early in the buying cycle. If you can influence the buyer's key purchase criteria in your favor early in the process, then you will have a much stronger chance of winning them later. Also, if you are not part of the consideration set early in the process, you may never be considered for the purchase.

Key Purchase Criteria—What do they want?

Once you've defined the personas you plan to address, you'll need to decide what's most important to them. For each persona, make a list of their key purchase criteria. In other words, what factors do they use to make a decision about what to buy? If you are selling cell phones, your customers might be thinking about price, technology, ease of use, compatibility with a network, design, size, weight, style, and other features they might want.

Once you have a good set of criteria identified, rank order the criteria from most important to least important.

Positioning vs. the Competition

The next step is to determine how well your product or service fits the needs of the persona. To do this, rank your own company on a scale of 1–7 on each of the key purchase criteria you listed above. Then do the same for at least two of your competitors. When you complete this exercise, you'll be able to see your own strengths and weaknesses, as well as the strengths and weaknesses of your competitors on the factors that are most important to a particular market segment.

The factors that enable you to win against your competition are your sources of competitive advantage. The factors that you lose on are weaknesses that you'll need to overcome. It's best when you win significantly on the things that are most important to your buyers. If you don't have competitive advantages on the things that are most important to your buyers, you may be at a competitive disadvantage. This may require a new product strategy, or the need to address a different segment that values the things that you offer.

Once you complete this process for one market segment, repeat the process for all of the other market segments you plan to address. If you find that the segments respond in the same way, you may find that you have too many segments, and you'll be able to group them together and use the same messaging for both of these segments.

Marketing Research

Many companies complete the process described above with input from their management, sales, customers, prospects, and marketing teams. The results are so much more powerful, however, when you validate all of your assumptions with actual survey data from customers in your market. You may think you know what's most important to them and how you compare to your competition, but it can be very revealing to see how your customers really think based on data from a survey or focus group.

Differentiated Messaging—How to leverage your market position

Once you finish the process of identifying your sources of competitive advantage, you'll be ready to start writing your messaging. By giving your copywriters a complete understanding of the market segments you are focused on, what's important to them, and exactly how you win against your competition, they will have what they need to create the headlines, messaging, and other content that's necessary to sell your products and services.

Planning: The Business Opportunity and ROI

In order to get in the Digital Marketing Zone, you need to tie your marketing investments to the organization's business goals to create a Return on Investment, or ROI. Most marketers can quickly calculate the investment part of the equation in terms of media or creative costs, but they have a hard time understanding the return. I've often heard marketers talk about the ROI in terms of clicks, social media mentions, press mentions, retweets, conversions, or some other marketing metric. While many of these metrics are important, they are not a return. A "return" is measured in money—period. If you can't calculate the return in terms of money, there is no ROI.

To calculate a true ROI, you need to connect the dots between the investment you make and the dollars you generate. This can be more or less difficult depending on your industry. If you are a B2B marketer, your marketing investments will generate leads, and you'll need to track these leads all the way through the sales process in order to determine which source of leads is most effective. For example, if you invest $10,000 in a campaign and you generate 100 leads, your cost/lead is $100. If your sales team closes 10 of these leads, you get 10 new customers, and you can measure the sales and profits from these transactions to help you calculate the ROI.

Once you have this level of tracking in place, you can calculate the ROI based on the money you make from each sale. If you make $1,000 from each sale, your ROI is 0%—you broke even. If you make $5,000 from each sale, your ROI is 400%. If you make $50,000 from each sale, your ROI is 4,000%.

The beauty of digital marketing is that you can track this at a much more detailed level than you can with traditional marketing. You can see which offers, keywords, campaigns, or messages produced these leads and sales, and spend more on those parts of your campaign. You can also cut your budget on campaign elements that do not produce results. By doing this you will not only be able to calculate the ROI, but improve the ROI over time by basing the return in the equation on real money.

In each area of your Internet marketing mix, there are many intermediate measures that you can use to tell if you are on the right track. Don't be confused. The only real measure of success that counts for most companies is producing more money for the organization.

Marketing Planning

Marketing's role in demand generation is not a support function but a core business function, just like sales, manufacturing, and distribution. It is marketing's responsibility to drive the leads, traffic, and website visits that are necessary for the company to be successful.

Marketing's demand generation work can be put on a quota in a way that is completely integrated with sales. If the sales team is responsible for creating 1,000 proposals over the course of the year, then marketing may be responsible for generating 10,000 leads to enable this sales activity. All of the core demand generation activities can be tracked and measured to make sure that marketing is fulfilling its core demand generation role to support the business.

High-performance marketing requires a very different mindset than the strategic, creative, public relations or brand thinking that many people associate with marketing. It requires a focus on campaigns with goals, budgets, and metrics that track results. It also requires planning that is linked directly to sales planning.

Steve's Marketing Planning Experience

Steve called me one day because he was concerned about his marketing campaigns. He was paying his agency $10,000 per month, but he didn't feel that he was getting the lead flow that he wanted to justify the investment. After asking a few general questions, I asked him to give me access to his analytics tools and marketing reports so that I could diagnose the problem. I quickly found that he was generating only 37 leads per month from the entire campaign and that the vast majority of the leads were coming from his website. His social media, advertising, and email campaigns were producing almost nothing. In addition, his website organic lead flow was flat through the year.

Steve went from a general feeling of unease about his current program to near-panic. Over the next few weeks, I built a new plan for growth based on specific activities that could drive results. Steve gained confidence in the new plan because of the deep analytics we provided, and eventually moved the entire account to Nowspeed. With the integrated plan in place, we were able to focus on the right things and dramatically improve his results. Within three months of starting the new program, we doubled his website traffic and lead flow. Even more important, Steve had a clear roadmap for how the campaign would continue to be successful. While there was still a lot of work to do in order to make his campaigns successful, the plan took away a lot of his anxiety and frustration, and moved toward the Zone.

Developing Marketing Plans

In order to be successful with your demand generation program, you need to create a marketing plan that is driven by results, not activity. How can you tell the difference? An activity-based marketing plan will describe what the marketing team will do, not what it will achieve. An activity-driven plan might include the following items in given month:

- Weekly email campaign to prospects
- Monthly e-newsletter to customers
- $10,000 ad spending
- Two press releases
- 50 posts on social media sites
- New white paper content on the website

To calculate some of these investments, you'll need to track the marketing team's time to determine what it costs to produce items that require a time investment, such as social media or new content. Once you

A results-driven plan might include the same items, but include goals and costs:

Program	Investment	Planned Impressions	Planned Clicks	Planned Leads	Planned Customers	Planned Revenue
Weekly email campaign to 50,000 prospects	$4,000	7,500	250	25	3	$15,000
Monthly e-newsletter to 5,000 customers	$1,000	1,250	50	10	2	$10,000
$10,000 ad spending on paid search	$10,000	500,000	5,000	500	10	$50,000
Two press releases	$2,000	N/A	25	5	1	$5,000
50 posts on social media sites to 5,000 followers	$2,000	25,000	100	10	1	$5,000
New white paper content on the website	$3,000	10,000	500	50	5	$25,000
Total	$22,000	543,750	5,925	600	22	$ 110,000

finish the month, you'll be able to add actual results and calculate your cost per lead, and cost per customer. Then you'll be able to adjust the plan, focusing on the items that made the most impact for the lowest cost.

Just as the sales team has a quota for the revenue they are accountable for each month, the marketing team also needs to be held accountable for driving demand. This demand can be measured and evaluated in order to help the business leaders make good decisions on moving the business forward.

The first step in building your plan is to benchmark each of your marketing actives to see where you stand. These metrics might include:

- Website—For each source:
  ○ Total visitors
  ○ Organic search visibility and traffic
  ○ Leads or sales
- Digital Advertising—For each channel:
  ○ Impressions
  ○ Clicks
  ○ Conversions—leads and sales
- Email—For each target audience:
  ○ House email list size
  ○ Potential list size that you could purchase
  ○ Click-through rate and conversion rate on emails sent
- Social Media—For each social media site:
  ○ Followers
  ○ Clicks to the website
  ○ Leads and sales

Once you have a good understanding of your metrics and how your activity turns into results, you're ready to build your annual marketing plan.

The goal of the plan is to leverage the top performing marketing channels to generate the most qualified leads and sales for each marketing dollar invested. To reach this goal, you will build a marketing campaign plan that demonstrates, month by month, how your marketing, lead generation, and sales objectives will be achieved. The plan will consider the performance of various activities that could be used to achieve the objectives of the campaign, including digital advertising, SEO, email marketing, social media marketing, website optimization, and email lead nurture. You'll also need to review existing content assets to identify gaps and create a plan for future content production.

When you have the data ready, the plan should look something like this: The plan starts in January with real data from all of your programs, and then predicts improvements based on the actions you'll take during the year. These actions might be building a new website to improve conversion rates, investing in SEO, buying a bigger email list, creating better content, or spending more money on advertising. All of these activities should tie directly to improvements in your plan and produce a positive ROI.

One you have the plan ready, you can use it as a living, breathing tool throughout the year to record your actual results so that you can learn whether or not your actions are working as planned.

Campaign Budget Decision Framework

One of the things you'll notice when you build your plan is that not all programs generate results evenly. Some marketing tools are significantly more effective than others. When clients want to know the most important things they can do to improve their lead generation program results, I tell them to do the ones that are most effective first, and keep doing them until they can't produce anymore. Then add activities to the marketing mix, in order from the best to the worst performers until the leads become too expensive to justify an ROI.

Visitor Planner	December	January	February	March	April	May	June	Summary
Digital Advertising	-	132	1,650	1,275	3,188	3,188	3,188	12,620
Website and SEO	5,011	5,154	5,304	5,461	5,627	5,800	5,983	38,340
Social Media	164	172	180	188	196	204	212	1,315
Nurture	-	12	15	15	31	39	68	180
Email	-	62	0	970	940	910	880	3,762
Total Visitors	5,175	5,532	7,149	7,909	9,981	10,141	10,330	56,216

Lead Planner	Dec	Jan	Feb	Mar	Apr	May	Jun	Summary
Digital Advertising	-	2	42	42	106	112	119	423
Website and SEO	34	31	32	33	39	46	54	269
Social Media	3	3	3	3	4	4	4	24
Nurture	-	1	1	1	2	3	6	14
Email	-	0	0	19	19	18	18	74
Total Leads	37	37	78	99	170	183	200	803

To do this, you need to start by getting common metrics on all of your marketing activities, such as the cost per lead or the cost per qualified lead and the number of leads or sales produced. Then sort the activities from best to worst. When we do this exercise for clients, we typically find that their website is the top performer, followed by organic search, paid search, and in-house email list programs.

Of course, you need to execute these programs well in order to get good results. You also can't ignore up-and-coming marketing techniques, such as mobile or social advertising. It's critical to build testing into your budget to find new techniques that can turn question marks into stars.

Back in the early 1970s, the Boston Consulting Group developed a concept for helping clients determine which product lines a company should put its resources behind. Markets were identified as high growth or low growth, and products were classified by whether they used cash or generated cash. "Stars" were promoted, "dogs" were divested, "cash cows" were harvested to support other initiatives, and "problem children" were monitored carefully in the hope that they would become "stars." But obviously the risk remained that they would turn out to be dogs.

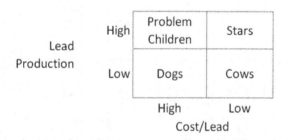

You can use this same approach to manage your portfolio of marketing programs. Build a 2X2 matrix with cost/lead or sales on the horizontal axis and leads or sales results on the vertical axis.

When you get your programs organized this way, you'll quickly realize where you'll need to focus your efforts. First, invest in the stars to see if these can pull in all of the leads or sales you need. Second, work on the cows. If you can find a way to get these low-cost techniques to build volume, you can turn them into stars. Next, focus on your problem children. These might be high producers that are expensive, but if you can bring the cost/lead down they can also turn into stars. Finally, think hard about the dogs. Do you really need them in your mix?

Additional Resources

Visit www.marketing-in-the-zone.com for additional resources to help you build your strategy and develop your plan.

- **Zone Situation Analysis, Objectives and Strategy Worksheet.** This worksheet will let you summarize your situation and your strategy on one page.
- **Zone Positioning and Segmentation Worksheet.** This tool will help you develop the key purchase criteria for your product or services that is most important to your target audience, and rank your company against your competitors in order to identify your sources of competitive advantage and help you develop your best messages.
- **Zone Marketing Planning Template.** This tool will allow you to benchmark your current campaigns and create a plan for improvement based on your activities and budget.

Part II
Accelerating your Marketing Organization

A Team in the Zone

E verything in marketing gets done by people, and if you want to get into and stay in the Marketing Zone, you have to work with the right people. People can create confusion that saps your strength, or they can energize you and move you to greater performance than you ever thought possible.

People that keep you in the Zone get things done and are accountable for their actions. They keep their promises and work cooperatively with others. They say, "Yes, and…" Not, "No, but…". They work with you to get rid of confusion and distractions so that you can stay focused on winning. They know where you are going and are signed up to go all the way.

The right people can make your work happy and fulfilling. To be in the Zone, it's not enough to work with people you enjoy, you have to work with people you trust, and who share your goals and values.

Building a Culture of Marketing Accountability

Marketing departments in many companies were one of the last major functions in business free of serious accountability. Every other core business function, from manufacturing to sales, was accountable for results, but the marketing department was often able to spend money without the same kind of serious scrutiny.

One reason for this is that many executives felt that marketing was a support function, similar to human resources or accounting, instead of a core business function directly in the path from production to customers. Core business functions include all of the elements that directly produce value from customers, such as purchasing, manufacturing, distribution, and sales. Each of these business functions must be held to a high standard and measured effectively if the business is to thrive. If your VP of Manufacturing decided to build a new factory and buy equipment, but could not predict how much he'd produce or at what cost, you'd soon be looking for a new VP of Manufacturing.

The sales department is also highly accountable. The company must count on the sales team to sell its quota in order for the company to be successful. The VP of Sales will generally break the company sales goals into regional, district, office, and individual quotas and measure results weekly, monthly, quarterly, and annually in order to make sure that they will be successful in making their goals. In addition, each core business function will track many other metrics that are important to their success. Sales will not only track orders, but also leads, proposals outstanding, proposal value, close rate, renewal rates, etc. in order to determine if they are on track to hit their goals.

In most organizations, marketing was treated as a support function without any of these metrics or tracking systems. Marketing is, of course, responsible for strategic decisions that cannot be tracked, such as pricing, product strategy, competitive positioning, messaging, and branding. These functions are important and make an enormous impact on the business if done correctly.

While marketing has a strategic role, it is also responsible for driving demand and creating marketing results. In the age of the Internet, it's possible to track the investments and hold marketing accountable for results. Because of these significant changes, you need a strong marketing team to bring you into the Zone.

Building a Strong Marketing Team

Finding the Right Team Members: Core Values

The first step in building a strong marketing team is finding people who match your core values. I've found that I'm always better off when I hire for attitude and train for skills. When I've done the opposite, I've always ended up with trouble.

At my company, we built a list of core values that have served us well. Our core values are: Trust and Respect, Service Excellence, Initiative, Innovation, and Integrity. In other words, we are looking for trustworthy people who we respect and who are respected by other members of our team. We want them to deliver excellent service to our clients all the time, and take initiative to get things done rather than wait to be told what to do. We live in a world of constant changes, so we also want them to innovate and bring new ideas whenever possible. We also want people of immense integrity who will always do the right thing for our company and our clients.

You may have a different set of core values, but it's important to define them and use those core values when you hire, coach, and evaluate your team members. Here's a tool you can use to evaluate every team member every quarter:

Team Member	Trust and Respect	Service Excellence	Initiative	Innovation	Integrity	Level
Tim	A	A	A	A	A	5
Susan	A	A	A	A	A	5
Bill	A	A	B	B	A	4
Julie	A	C	A	A	A	3
Scott	C	A	A	A	C	3

In this example you can see that Tim and Susan are doing a great job and we want to do everything we can to keep them. Bill is also doing a basically good job, but needs to be coached to take more initiative and be more innovative. Julia is a great person and is taking initiative, but she needs to improve her service quality dramatically if we are going to keep her. Scott is doing his work and is even delivering innovation, but he can't be trusted, so he might be the first to go. Every individual is different, but this tool can help you decide if you have the right people on your team to achieve your goals.

The Right Service Providers

While you are evaluating your team members, don't forget about your extended team of service providers. These people may be graphic artists, SEO specialists, website developers, writers, or others whom you rely on to get your work done. Here's a simple tool you can use each quarter to make sure you have the right team in place to help you be effective:

Service Provider	Core Values	Responsive	Quality	Results	Price & Value
Graphic Artist	A	A	A	A	A
SEO	A	A	A	A	A
Web Developer	A	A	A	A	B
Writer	C	A	A	A	A
Consultant	A	A	A	A	A

In this example you'll probably notice that your writer is not in tune with your core values, so he may not be a good fit and you may need to find another writer. Also, the web developer is expensive, so you may need to evaluate alternatives.

It's tempting to keep contractors even when they don't fit, and this tool can help you make sure that your extended team is the one you want to keep, and motivate you to make changes quickly when you need to.

Building a Level 5 Team

A strong team is more than just a smart group of people who fit your core values and can get things done. You need people who are knowledgeable about your industry, well trained, and have predictable processes that deliver consistent results. They also need to be able to leverage the massive amount of digital marketing data available in order to make good decisions and bring innovation to every area of your business. I call this a Level 5 Team. This type of team can take on any challenge and get results in the Zone. This type of team does not happen by accident, so you'll need to carefully consider how you can adjust your hiring and development systems to produce a Level 5 Team.

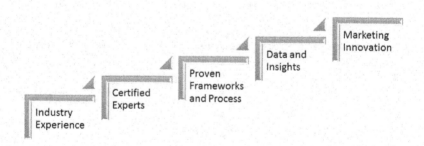

Industry Experience

The first step in building a Level 5 Team is to make sure your marketing team knows your business. Retail is different than telecommunications. Jewelry sales are different than big-ticket software sales. Every industry has its own language and its buyers think differently. Marketers can't be so focused on tactics and technical execution that they don't understand the business. One way to help get your marketing team in sync with your industry is to get them into the retail store, to a trade show, or in sales calls with your reps. They should also understand the nuts and bolts of the business by spending time on the shop floor, in the lab, or in your warehouse operations. By helping them fully immerse themselves in the details and language of your industry, you'll make them all better at communicating and driving results.

Certified Experts

In today's world, it's not enough to be experienced – you need to be technically great at what you do. In many areas of digital marketing, vendors and educators provide courses and testing to make sure you and your people know what they are doing. For example, in the early days of Google Adwords, we learned by trial and error and got good at managing campaigns through experience. Today, however, it's much easier to get better faster by completing all of the required Google certification course work, and then taking the required tests to get certified. Once you build your technology architecture in the next chapter, you will need to invest in training to get certified and build expertise with every tool and technology.

Proven Frameworks and Processes

It's not enough to be well trained and knowledgeable about the industry. You also need to have proven frameworks and processes to drive good marketing outcomes. The difference between training and a process is like the difference between completing a driver's education course and competing in NASCAR race. A 16-year-old with a new driver's license could get a NASCAR car around a track, but in a real competition, he or she would not stand a chance. The last section of this book will review frameworks for the most important areas of digital marketing. It's important to build a team that fully understands best practices and can deliver results that will help you win, not just participate.

Data and Insights

People who are well trained and get things done with strong processes in place also need to understand the role of data. It's easy to be so focused on doing your job that you don't want to complicate your life by analyzing data and using it to improve results. To get to this level, you need to set up a system to collect and analyze data, make regular decisions using the data, and document results. Building a strong culture of daily, weekly, and quarterly meetings that are fully informed with good data is an important way to help your team get comfortable with data in order to use it make sound decisions.

Innovation

When you are focused on driving good results and achieving your goals, it can be very difficult to innovate. Digital marketing technologies and best practices are changing so quickly that if you are not innovating, you are almost certainly falling behind. In order to innovate, you need to build a culture that allows people to investigate new software and new ways of doing things, as well as challenge existing processes. Innovation requires you to allow people to try things that may not work, but also to reward new and different thinking. You need people who can deliver results day in and day out, but also try new things. It can be difficult to manage innovation because things don't always work out the way you predict, but when innovation works, the results can be amazing.

Creating the Organizational Cadence

To keep your team working at peak performance in the Zone, you'll need to create an organizational cadence so that everyone is in sync. I call it a cadence, because the regular structure of good meetings keeps the pace moving forward the way you want, and keeps you from descending into marketing chaos. There are three elements of this meeting system: Quarterly Offsite, the Weekly Meeting, and the Daily Huddle.

Quarterly Meeting

Once every quarter, it's important to get all of the key marketing leaders away from the office for a full day to review the strategies, tactics, and plans in order to identify and deal with issues. This quarterly meeting will allow you to make sure you are focused on the right things and also doing things in the right way.

The meeting should start with some relaxed time to share personal good news so that people can get to know each other better. From there you should take time to review the marketing strategy to make sure nothing has changed and everyone is on the same page. Once this is complete, review your marketing scorecard, as well as the team, service providers, and software assessments. From there you can discuss the action plan and then move into departmental presentations in order to give each leader the chance to present in more depth their accomplishments for the quarter, issues, and recommendations for goals for the coming quarter. The meeting should conclude by prioritizing the action plan for the next quarter.

- Start with good news—personal and company headlines
- Review marketing strategy and discuss changes
- Scorecard results for the past quarter—identify issues
- Review the team, service providers and software assessments
- Review the action plan—progress and any issues

- Departmental presentations—accomplishments, issues and proposed goals
- Issues List—identify, discuss and solve
- Conclude by prioritizing the action plan for the next quarter
- Close on time

Weekly Meeting

The weekly meeting is where data and issues come together so that you can keep the organization moving forward. The meeting should be on the same day and the same time with a published agenda. You should also start and end as scheduled to respect everyone's time. The typical duration for a weekly meeting is one hour. Here is my recommended agenda:

- Start with good news—customer or employee headlines
- Scorecard results for the past week—identify issues
- Review the action plan—progress and any issues
- Issues List—identify, discuss and solve
- Conclude by reviewing the action plan for the next week
- Close on time

The bulk of the weekly meeting time should be spent discussing and resolving issues, not reading the data or discussing the action plan. By focusing on decisions and issues, you'll be able to remove obstacles and move the organization forward.

Daily Huddle

Some organizations find that it's helpful to have a daily huddle to keep everyone informed and on track. This is typically a short, standing meeting where each team member describes:

- What they did yesterday
- What they plan to do today
- Any issues

By keeping it short and letting each team member talk briefly, you can make sure that team members are aligned and working together. You can also quickly identify issues that come up so that you can deal with them and move forward.

Integrated Sales and Marketing

This chapter has been all about building an effective marketing team, but marketing does not exist in a vacuum. Since so much of marketing drives sales, it's critical to build alignment between the marketing and the sales team. When the sales and marketing teams are working effectively together, they have a common language, common goals, and shared data that helps both of them be more successful. They replace departmental rivalry with a cooperative attitude that puts both of them on the same team.

The first step is to create a common language. Often the problem between sales and marketing is that they have different meanings for the same word, or similar meanings for different words. Marketing may call a "lead" someone who has filled out a form on the website. Sales may only consider a "lead" real when they meet the BANT criteria of Budget, Authority, Need, and the company will make a decision during an acceptable Timeframe. At other times the sales team may consider a lead someone who is on a list that they already own or have just purchased. When there is no common definition of a lead, the marketing team may say that they passed 100 leads on to sales, but the sales team may say that they only got five real leads and the rest were "junk".

What's needed is a more detailed definition of each phase of the lead funnel so that the marketing and sales groups can clearly understand the process.

One set of definitions I've used successfully came from Sirius Decisions[6]. Their model creates a process that moves leads through the following steps:

- Inquiry
- Marketing Qualified—Leads that are not junk and worth contacting
- Sales Accepted—The sales person has looked at the lead and decided that it's worth pursuing
- Sales Qualified—The lead is qualified and becomes a sales opportunity because it meets the BANT criteria with the right budget, authority, need, and timeframe identified.

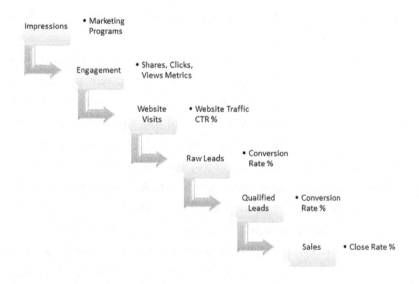

---

6   Source: Sirius Decisions. Footnote at www.marketing-in-the-zone.com/footnotes

With these common definitions in place, the marketing and sales teams can review leads to see which ones are moving through these steps, and which ones are getting stuck in the process. They can also calculate a cost per lead at each step of the process to help them make better investment decisions.

This can be extremely helpful in environments with very long sales cycles where it may take months or years to find out if a lead turns into a customer or not.

By creating a common language and a common set of goals, the marketing and sales groups can work together to achieve their goals.

Additional Resources

Visit www.marketing-in-the-zone.com for additional resources to help you build your strategy and develop your plan.

- **Zone Marketing Team Assessment:** Use this chart to identify your core values and rank each of your team members.
- **Zone Service Provider Assessment.** This tool will help you rate each of your service providers each quarter.

Part III

Accelerating your Marketing Technology Strategy

Technology is the glue that makes modern digital marketing work. If you do a good job selecting and managing marketing technology, it can make all of your campaigns easier to create and manage. If you select the wrong platforms or don't learn to use them effectively, you can create hell on earth. In this chapter I'll share the types of marketing technologies you should be using and review how to select and monitor your technology choices to keep this beast under control.

Over the last five years, we've seen thousands of new applications come on the market that let marketers build websites, manage ad campaigns, and even create content. Many of these applications are built as SaaS (Software as a Service), which means that they are often inexpensive, easy to install, and easy to use. With thousands of marketing software tools available, many marketing leaders are struggling to select and manage the right digital marketing software to drive campaign results. It's very common for marketers to live in a perpetual state of marketing tech confusion.

Here are some of the most common questions my clients are asking about marketing technology:

- How do I define my business needs for marketing software?
- What is the best software to meet my needs?
- What applications am I missing that could make a big impact on my business?

Before we talk about the best ways to select the right software, let's review the most important types of marketing software you'll need to build your confidence and drive successful campaigns.

The diagram below shows the most important categories and subcategories of Digital Marketing Software. You'll notice that there are 6 major categories and 45 subcategories in the Zone marketing technology architecture. There is lot of software in each category, and it can be a challenge to find the right applications in every category that are best for you. Once you select the software you need, it can also be a challenge to learn how to use each tool and get the most out of your software investment.

Marketing Software Categories

Here are the major marketing software categories and what to look for when you are selecting the right software for you.

Advertising

Advertising platforms allow you to manage the placement of ads across a variety of digital properties in order to drive traffic, engagement, leads, and sales. There are many choices for advertising management today to

Marketing Technology Architecture

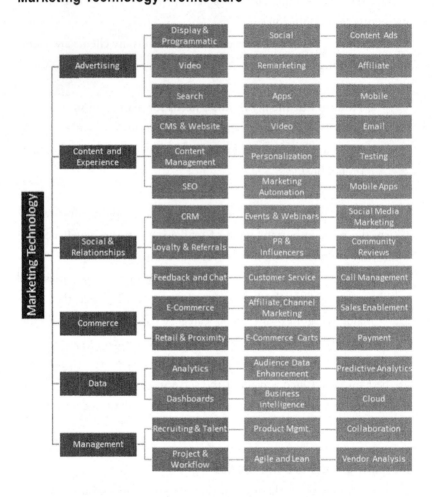

enable you to leverage search, social media, affiliates, websites, video, apps, and many other platforms to reach your target audience. These platforms will allow you to select your target, place advertising creative, spend advertising dollars, and monitor and track the results. Here are some questions to consider in building your advertising business requirements to share with vendors:

- How large is your advertising budget?
- Is your target audience reached best through search, social media, or other websites (or all of the above)?
- Is your goal brand awareness, engagement, traffic, leads, or sales?
- How much time do you have to invest in ad campaign management?

Content and Experience

Content platforms enable you to manage the content you've created, distribute content to your audience, attract content viewers, and even test the effectiveness of your content. This category includes website Content Management Systems (CMS), SEO, Marketing Automation, and email and video hosting. When you are considering content platforms, ask yourself the following questions:

- How much content do I have or plan to have in each area?
- How many pages are on my website?
- How automated would I like to make my content distribution?
- How personalized and dynamic should my content be to give a custom experience to each user?
- How extensively do I plan to test my content?

Social and Relationships

Social media and relationship platforms allow you to interact with a vast social community online through platforms like Twitter, LinkedIn, Instagram, and Facebook, and also enable interaction with individual prospects and customers through a Customer Relationship Management (CRM) system. When you are building your social and relationship technology framework, consider the following questions:

- How much content will I post on social media?
- How integrated will my CRM system be with my marketing systems?
- How will I manage interactions with influencers like analysts and the press?

Commerce

Commerce software enables you to sell online and collect payment, as well as manage shipping. This area also includes sales enablement software that gives your sales team important tools to communicate with prospects, develop proposals, or even sign orders. When choosing commerce software, consider the following questions:

- How integrated will your e-commerce system be with your traditional order management and accounting systems?
- How would you like to leverage online tools to let your sales teams be more effective?
- How would you like to integrate your retail or other local operations with your e-commerce software?

Data

Digital marketing systems produce big data, and you can learn a lot from this information. This component of the architecture includes analytics software, audience enhancement data, dashboards, business analytics, and the cloud infrastructure to enable all of the data. Key questions you should ask in this area include:

- What are the key performance indicators I plan to track each week and month?
- What types of additional questions would I like to ask with the data that's available?
- Who will be receiving the marketing reports and monitoring the dashboards each month?

Management

There are hundreds of management tools available to help you recruit, manage, and collaborate internally and externally. These tools can help you and your company dramatically increase your productivity. Questions to ask here include:

- How would I like to collaborate with my customers and prospects?
- How many people do I need to recruit this year?
- What is the best way to manage projects?

With dozens of categories and hundreds of products, these questions barely scratch the surface of building your business requirements, but they should get you thinking about ways that using the right marketing architecture can help you accelerate your marketing.

Software Inventory and Evaluation

In order to make sure you are getting all of the value you can from each software platform, it's important to evaluate your choices each quarter. By starting with an inventory of your software, you can quickly find overlaps between your tools and often save money by eliminating redundant licenses.

To get started, build a list of the tools you are using today, and organize them in the categories and subcategories listed above. Once you have this ready, rate each tool on the following criteria:

- Requirements Fit—Does this software help you do what you need to do?
- Value —Does the software deliver more value than it costs? You may see this value come in increase effectiveness, impact, or time savings.
- Innovation—Is this software adding new features to stay ahead of your competitors?
- Usability—Is the software easy to learn and use?
- Cost—How much does the product cost on a monthly or annual basis?

Additional Resources

Visit www.marketing-in-the-zone.com for additional resources to help you build your strategy and develop your plan.

- **Zone Marketing Technology Assessment:** Use this chart to identify your marketing technology providers and rank each one to find the partners that provide the most value.

Part IV

Accelerating your Content Marketing Program

Marketing Content in the Zone

Content can dramatically accelerate your marketing results, or it can act as boat anchor—slowing you down when you should be picking up speed. When you know all of your customer profiles intimately and have the marketing content they need, you can be confident that you are engaging them with the right information to move them through the buying process. Your videos, white papers, articles, web pages, and social media posts will get noticed and used, and you'll feel confident that the content engagement numbers you are measuring will translate into sales.

Many people I speak with, however, don't live like this. They don't really understand the gaps in the content they need, and they feel like they are constantly on the content treadmill, churning out article after article, with no end in sight. In addition, they can't connect the dots between the content they produce and the results in the business. The result is that they often don't care about the content and it ends up being poorly written or produced.

By rethinking your content strategy, you can take a step deeper into the Marketing Zone, and gain a new sense of confidence and energy as you create your content.

Content Marketing Introduction

Content marketing is everywhere. As the web and social media have become integral parts of all of our lives, large and small companies are using content to build engagement with both current and potential customers.

Developing great content is one of the most important functions of marketing. Providing excellent and relevant content to potential buyers establishes you as an expert and authority, and engages potential customers throughout the buying cycle. This creates brand loyalty, improves retention, focuses attention, and generates leads. Engaging new and existing customers by educating them is a great way to build relationships, and it helps you and your company become a thought leader and industry expert.

Consumer products companies as diverse as Kraft Foods and LEGO have been using content marketing for years to engage with customers, build their brands, and grow sales. Kraft started with recipe books and evolved into sophisticated websites and apps to help their loyal customers understand how to use food products such as Velveeta, Cool Whip and Jell-O in new and innovative ways. In the toy category, LEGO has a LEGO Club that produces a beautiful monthly magazine for LEGO fans and their parents. They also produce videos, games, and other content to make sure they are top-of-mind for their customers for every birthday or holiday.

Both B2B and B2C organizations are producing and promoting a large variety of content. Companies produce videos, white papers, articles, infographics, e-books, and more in order to engage potential customers at many points in the buying process.

Incredibly, 86% of marketers are using content marketing today[7]. A recent Content Marketing Institute surveys show that the most popular types of content are social media content, articles on a website, newsletters, blogs, events, case studies, and videos.

Susan's Content Marketing Program

Susan was the Marketing Director at a client that sold software to physicians to help them improve the cash flow from their practices. The company had been operating for several years and she hired us to improve website traffic and lead flow. We dove into the program, but the results came slowly. Organic search traffic grew slower than planned, and their cost per lead from advertising was higher than planned. The plan called for Susan to create weekly blog posts, monthly webinars, and three white papers, but she had been too busy to get this done during the first six months of the program.

At our second quarterly review, we showed flat results and told her that results would not improve until she got the content done. This was enough to get her fired up. She asked us to create the white paper, and she wrote the other pieces within 30 days. The results were dramatic. Organic Search traffic and Digital ad lead flow increased dramatically over the following quarter and continued to produce good results over the next year. Content was the key that turned the campaign around.

When she started producing content regularly and we were able to show consistent and strong results, she became a

---

7   Source: Content Marketing Institute. Footnote at www.marketing-in-the-zone. com/footnotes

happier client and I'm sure her feelings of stress were reduced. The right content helped her move into the Zone.

Content Marketing Strategy

Many organizations simply create a bunch of content, but it's important to move from just creating content to leveraging it as part of an integrated strategy. A good content marketing strategy will include designing the right content based on the needs of your audience, creating a manageable content program calendar, and promoting all of your content using social media and digital advertising in order to drive traffic, leads, and sales. Your strategy should also include ways to measure the results of your content marketing program so you can clearly demonstrate to the organization how you're making an impact.

How effective is your content marketing program? It's interesting that very few marketers feel that they are being effective in this area. According to the Content Marketing Institute, only about 8% of marketers rated themselves as very effective and 30% said they were somewhat effective. This means that only 38% of marketers felt like they are doing a great job with content marketing, and most marketers thinking they're mediocre at best[8]. This survey shows that few marketers feel they are operating in the Zone. When you are in the Zone, you have the confidence that you are doing great work and that it's making a difference.

---

8   IBID

Once you implement the program described in this chapter, you will have created a world-class content marketing program that's directly tied to your organization's marketing strategy. You will learn how to create the right content and develop the metrics to prove that it's effective, so that you can be confident that you are making a positive impact on your organization.

Many organizations struggle with creating the content they need. Here are six steps that will help you build a comprehensive content marketing strategy and create content that delivers results:

1. Identify your content marketing goals, determine what you are trying to accomplish, and define the business benefits that you're trying to achieve. In this step, you will also create the metrics you need to understand the impact you are making.

2. Review your website analytics, your competitor's websites, and the content you already have through a comprehensive content audit.

3. Understand your buyer's journey and the process they go through to identify what they want to buy and who they want to buy it from.

4. Create personas for the market segments you want to address using market segmentation techniques to figure out who your best customers are and how you can speak to their needs directly. To create personas, you will need to understand your ideal customers, how they make buying decisions, the questions they ask, and the content they need.

5. Create an editorial calendar so that you have a solid plan in place to create the content for your program. This will include creating a specific plan for who's going to write or create the content you need for your program.

6. Leverage your content for results. This includes using SEO, digital advertising, email, and a number of other programs to build your brand, engage with your customers, generate leads, and ultimately grow sales.

Content Marketing Goals

There are many things you can accomplish with your content marketing program, so it's important to focus on the right goals for your organization. According to one study, one of the most popular goals for content marketing programs is lead generation. If your organization markets and sells to other businesses, you're most likely going to be using your content to drive leads.

Another important goal for most content marketing programs is thought leadership, which establishes your company as a leader in the market. The third most popular goal is brand awareness, which involves breaking through the clutter to build your brand and grow the overall reputation of your organization. Other goals you may consider could include nurturing your leads, driving sales, and building website traffic.

After you've determined your overall goals, you'll need to turn each general goal into specific metrics that you can measure and that your content marketing strategy can accomplish. In a recent survey, when marketers were asked about their most important metrics, they answered that they use website traffic, sales increases, social media sharing metrics, and time spent on the website to measure success[9].

If you want to increase SEO visibility, you should set goals for specific keyword visibility and for increasing organic SEO traffic. If you want to increase social media engagement, you should set goals for how many followers or fans you want. It's important to be as specific as possible about how you want to make a difference. As you plan your social media content marketing goals, you should first create a benchmark to see how

9   IBID

much traffic is currently coming to your website from social media, so that you can plan your improvements.

If you want to increase the effectiveness of your digital advertising program, consider what you want your new conversion rates to be, how many leads you want, or how you want to change the cost per lead. If your goal is to improve your email program, you may want to increase your email click-through rates, open rates, or conversion rates.

There are so many goals that you can focus on, it's best to get specific and create targets for yourself in each of these areas, so that you can demonstrate to the business that content marketing is having an impact.

Analytics Tools

In order to measure your success, you'll need to install and use the right tools. Google Analytics is an excellent tool to help you understand the traffic that's coming to your website and the source of that traffic.

Google Search Console is a great way to see your website the way that Google sees it. Among many other things, it shows your keyword visibility so that you can see the impact of your content marketing program on SEO.

Social Media management tools like Hootsuite and Spout Social can also be helpful to let you understand how your content marketing program is impacting social media followers and engagement.

Content Audit

Before you create a solid content marketing strategy, you have to do your homework and determine what you know, what you have, and what you need. To get started, you should conduct a content audit to understand the content assets you already have in your organization.

As part of your content assessment, remember to review your Google Analytics or other analytics tools and see what content is the most popular and effective, what gets the most mentions and retweets in social media, and which content gets shared and liked in your industry. Before you trust the raw statistics you find, remember that that popularity can be a self-fulfilling prophecy, since the most popular content may be the content that has been featured or promoted the most, not necessarily the content that is the best quality.

You may have been producing articles, white papers, or videos for years, but you may not feel like your content is high enough quality, or that it is addressing all the different market segments that you need to communicate to. As you do a content inventory, remember to rate the quality of your content and determine how it can fit into your plan.

Next, look at your competitors. What content do they have? Do they have more than you, or less? Are you playing catch up, or do you have an opportunity to go way beyond them in terms of your content marketing program? When you look at your competitors, try to understand the topics that are important to them and the types of media are they using.

While you're looking at all this data, don't forget to talk to your customers and your salespeople. Often, your salespeople or senior executives can tell you a lot about what they're hearing, and what they're learning from customers and prospects about the content, issues, and media.

Next, review industry research and look at the topics that are most important to industry analysts. Analysts have their finger on the heartbeat of new topics that can be important as you put your plan together.

Once you've done your homework and understand the topics that might be part of your content marketing plan, you need to look at your own team to assess the skills you have internally to create new content. Do you have great writers on staff? Do you have a video department? Do you have great people that can produce graphics and infographics? If you don't have internal resources, you may need to find vendors or contractors to help you create all of the content you want as part of your plan.

Align Content to the Buying Process

In B2B organizations, content like white papers, articles, and webinars fits well in the awareness phase. They help people understand the problem, come up with potential solutions, and think about how to address the situation.

In the evaluation phase, people are more interested in case studies and social media content to help them understand how other people actually solved their problems with a particular product. They also look at product information and company information to understand who makes the best products or delivers the best services.

In the purchase phase, they might be interested in a live demo or trial, or an assessment to get some experience with the product before they make a final purchase decision.

Once you have a solid understanding of the buying process, you can plan your content more specifically. For each piece of content, you should ask yourself which stage of the buying process it addresses. Is it of the quality and timeliness that you really need? By aligning your content with the way people actually buy, you will be able to ensure you have all of the right content you need to win new customers.

Planning Your Content: Editorial Calendar

Once you create your buyer personas, you can begin to plan out the content you will need to produce in order to help your buyers make a buying decision. Your buyer may want to read white papers, blogs, how-to content, and educational content in the awareness phase. In the evaluation phase, you may want to offer case studies, samples, or product and company information that your buyer needs to properly evaluate your products and services.

Persona: Patricia – Marketing Manager		
Awareness	**Evaluation**	**Purchase**
White paper	Case study	Live Demo
Blog Article	Sample	Free Trial
How-to	Product Info	Assessment
Education Issues	Company Info	Coupon

In the purchase phase, you may want to offer specific engagement tools such as a live demo, a free trial, free assessment, or a coupon that the buyer needs in order to make a positive decision for you. As you plan your strategy and editorial calendar, remember that it all needs to be focused on your specific buyer personas so that you can tailor it to their specific needs.

Now that you have a plan and a strategy, you can focus on actually creating all of the content. The average B2B marketer uses twelve different content types, so how do you create all of this content efficiently and effectively? To get started, it's best to use tools that are the most popular, such as social media, articles, newsletters, blogs, case studies, and videos.

To make content creation efficient and effective, you can also start with core ideas around your products, thought leadership issues that you want to address, client stories, or even events. Once you produce your core content, you can write more than one article about it and create derivative content and social media posts.

For example, if you've gone through the hard work of putting together an important thought leadership piece, the next step is to leverage that core content in as many different forms as possible. One way you can do this is by producing one solid white paper and then turning that into a series of articles. You can then use the articles to create shorter blog posts. From there, you repurpose the content for your website, use it in an email campaign, and leverage it for your digital ad campaign. You can also tweet about it, produce a short video, and even turn it into a podcast.

If you think about your editorial calendar as one continuous stream of content production, you can take one project, such as a white paper, and leverage it in many different ways to produce a wide variety of content for your program.

Once you understand how to use leverage to produce a wide variety of content, you can do the detailed work of creating the editorial calendar to get ready to produce the content itself. The editorial calendar is basically a spreadsheet or project plan to take all of these different ideas we've discussed so far, and put them into a detailed plan.

Your editorial calendar (see the chart blow) should include the topic, type of content, due date, the creator's name, the buying stage, and the persona to which it is addressed. For example, if I want to

Due	Who	Buying Stage	Persona	Type	Topic	Execution
Oct. 1	Susan	Awareness	Patricia - 20s	Blog	Financial Planning	Blog, Social Media
Oct. 7	Bob	Awareness	Joe & Deb - Married	Blog	529 Plans	Blog, Social Media
Oct. 15	David	Awareness	Harry – 50+	White Paper	Retirement Plans	Website, Ads, Email
Oct. 23	Susan	Awareness	Jeff - CEO	Blog	Diversification	Blog, Social Media
Oct. 15	Karen	Evaluation	Joe & Deb - Married	Case Study	Your Company Difference	Email Nurture, Website

build an awareness-level piece targeted at Harry, I might create the task and assign it to David. The plan is to produce a white paper on retirement plans, and we're going to leverage that through a number of channels, including our website, digital advertising, and our email campaigns.

The plan also shows that we want Karen to write an evaluation-stage-level piece targeted at Joe and Deb. The piece is going to be a case study focused on company differentiation, and we're going to leverage that on our email campaign, website, and blog. With this simple tool, you can create a detailed plan to describe exactly who's doing what, so that you have a fully functional editorial calendar.

Editorial calendars are an often talked about, but little used technique, so I'd encourage you to get very specific in your plan to determine exactly who's going to do what in building the content so that you can get it all done.

Ideas for Creating Content

At times, it might be difficult to think of new ideas for content, so here are a few techniques that might help you get new ideas.

- Interview your customers.
- Survey your readers to find out what they are interested in.
- Highlight case studies and customer stories.
- Share success and failures.
- Tell a personal story.

These are just some ideas that can help you come up with good content creation ideas.

Here are the most common types of content that you may use in your content marketing program.

White papers

White papers provide customers with information about, or solutions to, problems they might have. They serve in establishing thought leadership and expertise by showing how you can help solve a problem. A good white paper will capture the reader's attention and draw in a large audience. The best white papers address the "pain" of your target audience in a powerful and provocative way. They can be focused on strategic issues or very tactical tips depending on your target audience.

Webinars

Like white papers, webinars provide information that promotes thought leadership. Webinars, however, offer a valuable chance to interact with potential and existing customers as well as others in your field. A good webinar has many of the characteristics described above, but it also should have engaging speakers.

The best webinars will feature an industry celebrity who people want to hear from and get close to. Imagine how differently you feel about going to a webinar featuring Larry Page, CEO of Google, vs. one of its many product managers. The actual content from one of their product managers may be more detailed and more useful to you, but don't discount the value of using a celebrity in your webinars. Once webinars are produced, they can also be recorded and reused as offers and additional content. The content can also be turned into a white paper and provide even more leverage.

Case studies

Case studies can provide valuable content about your company and the impact that it can make on customers. They demonstrate your problem-solving skills and the impact you've had on real situations. The power of the case study is that it tells a story. Most people find it much easier to understand a story than a list of facts, features, and action items. The story can also have an emotional element or sense of suspense to make it more effective. People understand complex information presented in stories better, and they are also better at remembering stories.

Video

Video use on the Internet has grown exponentially over the past few years. It has the ability to tell a story and communicate information in a powerful, creative, and emotional way that cannot be matched by text or even live events. Video can be used to tell customer stories, educate your audience, or sell a product. It can be used alongside other content, such as when you include a one-minute promotion in front of a white paper, or as a replacement for a detailed product data sheet.

Both professionally shot video and personal video is acceptable on the Internet. Personal video has an amateur quality that people often find to be more real and authentic than the slick commercials seen on TV. These can also be much less expensive to produce so that you can create more of them. If you choose to use personal video, make sure that the sound and video quality is good enough so that your users are not annoyed by the video, and they can still get significant value.

Comparison Guides

A guide to help users make decisions about the types of products they need is a very powerful type of content. People often struggle with finding all of the information they need to make an informed purchase decision and need documents that put all of the issues together for them in an easy-to-use format. Keep in mind that a comparison guide can be written at several levels to help people at each stage of the buying cycle.

In the awareness phase, people need help understanding the types of solutions available. An example of this type of guide would be "Road Bikes vs. Mountain Bikes." In the consideration phase, people need help understanding how your products are different than others. An example of this type would be, "Trek vs. Cannondale—Who has the strongest frame?" In the purchase phase, people need help understanding which of your products to choose. An example of this would be, "How to choose the right road bike for you." Comparison guides are helpful because they address the core needs of the reader during the right phase of the buying cycle.

Leverage Your Content for Results

Content makes all of your digital marketing programs easier. From social media to SEO to email and digital advertising, this section will help you understand how and where to leverage your content.

Social Media

Once you've produced your content, one of the first things you can do is promote it on social media channels. You can push it out on Facebook, Twitter, YouTube, LinkedIn, Google +, Pinterest, and more. To do this, you will need to host the content on your website, blog, or another place on the Internet, and then create a post and link back to it. The links will be visible to your followers and fans, and many people will see them. Of course the more fans you have, the more traffic and engagement you will have. The top social media sites are Facebook, Twitter, YouTube, Instagram, Snapchat, LinkedIn, Google+, and Pinterest, but don't ignore some of the other social bookmarking sites such as StumbleUpon and Tumblr, that can provide great links back to your content.

SEO

There are many ways you can use your content to boost your organic search engine rankings (SEO). The most highly rated tool in SEO is content creation. Since Google has gotten better with their search algorithm, they have weeded out a lot of bad content and links.

With recent Google changes, content creation stands out as the best SEO technique.

As you put your content on your website, you should include important keywords on the body copy as well as other html tags to make it look exactly like what the search engines want to see so that it can be effective for SEO purposes. You can also place your content on other sites or blogs and use it to link back to your website.

Email

Email is one of the most popular and important digital marketing techniques and a great way to leverage your content. If you have a multi-touch email campaign, you can use the buying process strategy that we've discussed to plan your email campaign content, so it will nurture prospects through the buying cycle. You might want to create a first-touch email that is awareness-oriented, in which you feature a white paper or webinar. Touch two might be an "evaluate" oriented piece that's more case study oriented or product oriented, and in touch three, you might send a free trial offer or "get started" offer.

You can, of course, leverage the core content you have by targeting it at different personas. In order to do this, you will need to segment your house email list so that you can send specific content to specific people through the buying cycle. This will allow you to customize the email copy to the persona you are addressing, so that it feels personal. Segmenting the list and sending personalized email is going to dramatically improve your email marketing program.

Digital Advertising

The last technique we'll discuss is leveraging your content for digital advertising. Strong content featured on well-designed landing pages can dramatically improve the results of your advertising programs. You can promote content using Google Adwords Search and Display Ads, and also using social media ads through sites like Facebook and LinkedIn. You may want to use digital advertising to promote content such as white papers that can drive leads, or just get more engagement with your video or infographics content. The chapter on digital advertising will give you much more detail on strategies to drive good results.

I've seen advertising programs that leverage good content increase conversion rates by 500%. It can make a huge impact in your program if you're promoting strong content versus just building traffic to your website. You can get more leads, and it can dramatically increase the ROI of the program.

Content Marketing Strategy Summary

This six-step content marketing strategy will help you create a world-class program that is efficient and effective, and makes a measurable difference to your organization. Remember to start with your content marketing goals, and then do your homework to analyze your buyer's journey so that you can build personas. When you complete this work, you can build a very specific editorial calendar to get the work done. Once you have a plan, you can leverage your content in every part of your digital marketing program. By following this strategy, you will move into the Zone with a comprehensive content marketing program that will make a big impact in your organization.

Additional Resources

Visit www.marketing-in-the-zone.com for additional resources to help you develop your content marketing plan.

- **Zone Content Planning Tool.** This chart will help you develop a detailed content plan for each persona and each phase of the buying cycle.
- **Zone Content Calendar.** Once you have the content identified, this chart will enable you to build a calendar and a schedule to get the content created.

Part V

Accelerating Your
Website Performance

Websites in the Zone

Your website should be the place where all of your marketing ideas, content, goals and messages come together to create a powerful resource for your audience. Your current and potential customers should be able to use it to clearly understand your products and services and get the information they need to do business with you.

I've found that many people are confused about their website. Some see it as a simple brochure, and others see it as a place to display cool designs or content without much in-depth information. Others don't think its relevant at all, and are satisfied with having a design with content that's three, five, or even 10 years old.

When your website is in the Zone, you can be confident that all of your target audiences will be able to get the information they need in a quick and easy way, and have a clear path to the next step in doing business with you. You'll also be able to document the success of the website with clear metrics about traffic, engagement, and leads. In addition, you'll have a clear understanding of where the website fits into the rest of your digital marketing program.

I hope this section will put you on a path to getting into the website Zone.

Jack's Website

Jack wanted a new website. As head of sales and marketing at a mid-sized tech firm, he had the nagging feeling that his website was out of date, did not communicate all of his best messages, and was not driving leads. He was also frustrated that it was hard to make changes, add content, and his organic search traffic was also very low.

I looked at the website and found that it had been developed four years ago and was still in HTML, so there was no content management system to make it easy to update. The design also looked dated, and did not reflect their high-tech image or latest messages. I also saw that it was entirely in English, even though the company had significant customers in China. The few content offers available on the site were buried deep and the SEO tags were badly implemented.

We built Jack a beautiful new website in WordPress to address these shortcomings. The new site featured a modern design in English and Chinese, and was easily visible on mobile devices. Since it was designed in WordPress, it was easy to update. It featured white papers on the home page with well-designed landing pages which dramatically increased lead flow.

Jack appreciated the new website, which took a lot of friction away from his ability to communicate with current and potential customers. He also became much more positive and optimistic about his company since his vision was now in sync with his website.

Website Strategy

In order to create a high-performance website, you need to fully optimize the experience for your audience so that they take the actions you want. Websites often have many audiences, such as existing customers, potential employees, and even investors. In this chapter we will focus on potential customers as the most important audience for the website.

Most B2B companies want their website to convert visitors to leads, which usually happens when visitors fill out a form and give you their contact information, start a chat session, or call on the phone. For most B2C websites, the goal is to move the visitor quickly through the buying process so that they will make a purchase.

The marketing goal of the website in general, and the home page in particular, is to present offers that are appropriate to users and encourage them to learn more by clicking to a landing page and entering their contact information, or going to a catalog page to make a purchase, or making a phone call. In order to do this effectively, everything about the site must be fully aligned – from the messaging to the design, the content, and especially the offers.

Here are the steps you'll need to take to create an effective website:

Website Strategy → Architecture → Design → Development → Launch

Strategy, Brand, and Messaging

The first element to consider about your website is the way it reflects your brand and messaging. Nothing is more frustrating than going to a website and hunting around for several minutes before you figure out what the company does.

It's critical that your headlines, photos, and copy clearly describe your category as well as the products and services you offer. It's also critical to select a design style with graphics that complement your brand and messaging to help your users quickly understand your company and the products and services you offer.

We've all visited websites that make it very difficult for their users. I recently visited a company with a large aloe plant on the home page and general statements about their commitment to client satisfaction. It took me several minutes to see that they were in the business of taking over and managing company mailrooms and other facilities.

Another website I visited recently showed a picture of a man with an umbrella under a shower of paper falling all around him. This website was promoting an online translation service, but it was very difficult to make the connection between the photo and the headline and service.

In the chapter on Marketing Strategy, I describe the process of understanding your target audience and creating personas that make it easy for you to think about your target market. This same process can be used to help you build your website. If you can put yourself in the shoes of these buyer personas, it's much easier to see the website from their perspective and design it around their needs instead of your own.

A well-designed website has clear messaging that anyone can understand within a few seconds. In addition, the layout and graphics will support the messaging and make it easy to understand what you do and how you can help the visitor get what they want.

Information Architecture

In order to build a high-performance website, you need to have an effective information architecture. The information architecture describes the layout of the website, including the site structure and how the pages are linked to each other. This will ultimately be turned into the navigation structure, links, and offers on each of the pages. The information architecture is critical since it will determine the size of the site and all of the content that needs to be created for the site. Many firms also build the SEO plan into the information architecture of the site.

Getting the information architecture right is critical to making the website design work. In the process of creating it, you will make decisions about how much content to put on the site and how to organize it. As you organize the content, you should follow basic rules that make it easier for people to find your content. For example, drop down menus with more than six or seven items are hard to use. If you have a lot of content on one page, you may want to break it into more than one page.

As you make decisions about the type of content, the amount of content, and its organization, you'll be able to determine how to organize the menus of the website to make it easier to navigate the site. Many sites have four or more levels of menus on each page to make it easy to find content and navigate to the right place.

Home Page and Secondary Page Design and Architecture

In addition to the site architecture, it's important to carefully think through the home page and secondary page architecture. By this I mean the layout of the content on the pages and the placement of offers and your calls to action.

The home page structure is especially important, since most of your users will start there. The home page gives you the opportunity to present key messages, news, product offers, and information offers such as white papers, demos, and videos. Since the location, color, size, and presentation of each item on the page will determine how visible it is and how much traffic it gets, it is very important to think about what's most important to you.

Do you want people to learn about the product, or select an offer? Do you want people to read the CEO's letter to shareholders, or read your press releases? If you want leads, you'll need to make your best offers very prominent and make it easy for users to get them. If you want sales, you'll need to make it easy to buy.

For example, if the primary goal of the home page is to drive users to see a demo and download a trial of your product, you should present your offer in the most visible place with the most eye-catching design possible. If you want people to sign up to get a discount coupon, make that offer the most prominent.

This thinking should also apply to the secondary pages on the website. If you do your SEO job well, you'll be generating more and more traffic directly to interior pages of the site since the users will be bypassing the home page when they come from a search link. It's very important to think about how users will experience your site if they go directly to these secondary pages. Will they understand your business and where they are on the site? Will they be able to navigate easily to other parts of the site? Will they find an offer that engages them and makes it easy for them to buy something or give you their contact information? Those are the challenges you'll need to overcome as you create your secondary page designs.

Integrating Offers into the Website

As you create your architecture, it's important to think deliberately about which offers to place on each page of your website. By placing relevant offers on each page, you'll increase the click-through rate and conversion rate, and improve the overall effectiveness of your website. As tempting as it can be to offer many things on each page, you can actually confuse your website users with too many offers. It's best to select the most appropriate offer for each page on the site and then test other relevant offers over time to see if you can improve your conversion rates.

In addition to content about your company, your products, and your services, you should also include other content to make your website valuable to people and position you as a thought leader. This content might include:

- Blog
- Directory
- Glossary
- White papers
- Articles
- Video
- Infographics

Your website is the natural place to showcase the thought leadership content you create, so plan for a resources section of your website that is alive with new content that you create and post frequently. The easiest place to start is with a blog where you write articles at least weekly. The resources section of your website will allow you to engage your users, build your brand, and get more SEO visibility since search engines love fresh content.

Selecting a Content Management System

Once you launch your new website, you'll need to make frequent changes as your business changes and evolves. A content management system (CMS) is software that enables you to easily manage and maintain a website once it has been created. It works by presenting your content through a series of templates for the website design.

In a CMS, all of the content for each page is in a database and only displayed to the user through the template when they visit the site. This means that you can easily make changes to the content and certain other site elements quickly and easily without redesigning the page. You can also entrust site editing to people with little HTML experience, since it is difficult to break the templates.

Popular content management systems like WordPress and Squarespace make it easy and less expensive to create a beautiful and effective website that can be easily managed. When you work with a product like WordPress, you can either create a custom design or work with an existing template. If you choose a template approach, your design will be limited, but you will get many features at a very low cost. Choose your template carefully, because once you build your website in a template, you will be committed to it for a long time.

Before you select a CMS, however, makes sure it meets all of your requirements. If you are building a complex e-commerce website or have thousands of pages of content, then WordPress may not be best for you. There are many commercial CMS products that have robust features and may be a better long-term alternative.

Building a Mobile-Friendly Website

Since many people today browse the web from smartphones and tablets, you should design your website to be as easy to use on these devices as on a PC or Mac. In the past, companies would build two different websites, one for mobile and one for desktop users. Today, a modern CMS allows you to build using "responsive design" so that the website automatically reformats based on the size of the user's browser. To do this, you will need to build templates for each size of browsers you expect to visit your site. Many companies build for three sizes including smartphones, tablets, and PCs.

By doing this you can deliver an excellent user experience for mobile users, while not taking the time and expense to build and maintain two completely separate websites. Managing content is easier with this approach too, since if you make a change in your content, it will instantly appear in both the mobile and PC version. Search engines reward you for showing mobile content correctly, so building a responsive website should also increase your SEO visibility.

Your website will be the core of your digital marketing program, so it's critical to take the time to do it right. By starting with your brand, developing a strong information architecture, and creating an excellent design, you will lay the foundation for a strong website program.

Landing Pages

Landing pages are where "conversions" happen. A conversion may be someone completing a form to give you their contact information before downloading content, or it may be an e-commerce purchase from a catalog. Well-designed landing pages can improve conversion rates tenfold compared to poorly designed pages, so it's critical to create them with care and use best practices to get the best results possible.

Even before you start to think about the design and copy of a landing page, it's important to put yourself in the shoes of the person who will be "landing" there. Are they responding to an email you sent to them, or are they responding to a search marketing ad? Are they visiting after exploring your website, or is this their first experience with you? In order to create the best landing pages possible, use the work you did on personas to make sure you get the message right.

If they are coming from your website to a landing page, you should make the experience consistent with the rest of the website. It should include all of the website's navigation to make it easy for them to move around the site, since you don't want them to feel as though they are leaving your website when they respond to an offer. It should also include the entire brand and core design elements of the website to deliver a consistent user experience.

If the landing page is a link from the website, you'll need to include information on the offer on the landing page, but you'll need less information to build trust and sell the company itself, since they are coming to this page from another page on the site. On the other hand, if the landing page gets a significant amount of organic website search traffic directly from the Internet, then you'll need more content in order to build trust just as you would if they were coming from an online ad.

Build Trust

If people arrive on your landing page directly from an online ad, you'll need to build trust and make sure they understand who you are and how you can help them. You'll not only need to sell the offer, but also communicate information about your company. No one will want to give you their contact information or buy from you if they are not sure want you'll do with the information. These trust building strategies are especially important if you have a brand that is not well-known. For example, it's easier to trust IBM or Coca Cola than it is to trust Bob's Consultants or Ben's Software.

There are several ways to build trust on a landing page. First, clearly tell the visitor who you are and what business you are in. You can also build credibility by showing them who your other customers are, and giving them quotes or testimonials. It's also important to highlight your privacy policy and let them know that you won't sell or give away their contact info. No one wants to feel that they are going to join a SPAM mailing list just for downloading a white paper.

Remember that you'll need do this in a very short space, so be brief. On a landing page the only space that matters is "above the fold", which is the visible part of the screen that a user sees when they arrive on your page. In many cases, it's unlikely that user will scroll down and see the rest of the page, so make sure you give them everything they need at the top of the page.

Sell the Offer

When creating a landing page, it's important to focus on only one thing. Internet users are easily distracted, and if you give them more than one thing to do, they will easily lose focus and move on. Even though you need to build trust, as I discussed above, don't include so much information on your company, products or customers, that you encourage them to move on before they "convert."

Landing Page Design Principles

When you start to design the landing page, make sure that the offer is clear and tangible. The graphic should make the value of the offer easy to understand. The headline and subhead should position the offer and make it easy to understand what you get. Most importantly, the form needs to be placed above the fold and be easy to fill out so that the user can get what they want. Following are some of the most common elements of landing page design:

- Layout—The entire layout should be easy to see and use within the screen users see when they arrive at the page.
- Mobile Design—The mobile design can allow more scrolling, but since space is limited, the offer should be very clear and the call to action should be obvious.
- Form Placement—The form should be on the page, above the fold, and at the top right of the screen. People generally read from left to right, so they should read about what they get before they are asked to fill out a form to get it.
- Form Length—The form should be as short as possible, but include all of the information you need to move the lead to sales. If this is an e-commerce transaction, you can break it up into separate pages to make each step easy to fill out.

- Make the offer tangible—If you are selling a product, include a picture, video, and enough information to help them make a purchase decision. If the offer is an information asset such as a white paper, then include a picture and something about the offer to help them understand how valuable it is.
- Headline and Subhead—The headline and subhead copy is important, since people need to be able to very quickly understand the offer and what they will get out of it.
- Copy—The copy should be short and easy to read to help the users quickly understand the offer and make a decision to request it.
- Navigation—If the user is coming from an ad, there should be minimal navigation so that they are not distracted and will move forward to get the offer.
- Call to Action—Instead of a "Submit" button, include a phrase like "Download Now" to encourage them to move forward.
- Trust Language—Include a short summary of your privacy policy such as, "We promise not to sell or share your contact information with anyone."

By using these principles, you'll be able to write and design a landing page that performs well. Keep in mind that all of these items can be tested to improve the results.

Website Analytics

Today's website analytics tools can provide you with a huge amount of data on what's happening on the website. You can get very detailed data on visits, page views, clicks, and conversions. You can also see where the traffic is coming from by referring website and often by keyword.

This data can tell you very important things about the effectiveness of your marketing programs and help you answer key questions such as:

- How effective are your home page and your landing pages?
- How effective is your website information architecture?
- How effective is your search engine optimization program?
- How effective is your social media marketing program?
- How effective is your email campaign?
- How effective is your content?
- How effective are your paid search or online advertising programs?
- What is not working well on the website?

Understanding your website analytics data is critical to helping you measure the ROI of your marketing programs and building a high-performance website.

When you start to use a tool like Google Analytics, it's easy to get lost in the overwhelming amount of data instead of focusing on what matters. While it might be interesting to know what percentage of your users are still using Internet Explorer 6.0, it's more important to know which websites are referring traffic and driving conversions, or which pages are driving the most conversions.

Once you determine the metrics that are most important, you can build a dashboard that summarizes those metrics and helps you quickly find the data you need.

Website Analytics tools are limited by the type of data they can get. There is a lot of data available, but the most important data I like to see includes:

- Traffic Sources—Where did the traffic come from and which traffic converted best?

- Visits to Pages—How many visitors went to each page?
- Goal Conversions—How many people converted to the goals you set?
- Referring Sites—Where did users come from?
- Geography—What countries, states, and cities did they come from?

You generally cannot see who came to your site unless the user provides their contact information. You also cannot see where they go after they leave your site.

Rather than focusing on what each metric means on the reports, I'd recommend that you focus on the decisions you want to make about your website each month, and then look at the data that can help you make those decisions. When you are building a high-performance website, you need to focus on:

- Home Page Performance
- Landing Page Performance
- Search Engine Optimization
- Social Media
- Email
- Paid Search or Digital Advertising

Home Page Performance

The goal of your home page is to clearly communicate your brand and product information, and then strategically lead people to learn more about your products, your company, and download an offer or buy something. Even though you may have many links on your website to news, events, customer stories, and other things, you should decide what you really want prospects to do from the home page and then track this metric to see if that's happening as you expect.

By measuring the click-through rate (CTR) from your home page to your product pages and your offer landing pages, you'll be able to see if the home page is doing its job effectively.

Landing Pages

The goal of your landing page is to convert the user to download something in exchange for their contact information, or to buy something. You can measure this by looking at the goal conversion rate for each of your landing pages. If you find that one landing page is converting more traffic than another, you can often increase the lead flow of your website simply by featuring the landing page with the highest conversion rate in the most prominent position.

Search Engine Optimization (SEO)

In the chapter on SEO, I discuss many ways to measure the effectiveness of your efforts to improve organic visibility. Website analytics give you an important perspective on your efforts and will help you see if the time and effort you are putting into SEO is making a difference.

Website analytics will tell you which organic search keywords are actually driving traffic to your website, which pages they are going to from their search, and if they are converting to one of your goals when they get there.

Google hides some of the information on organic search keywords, but you can still infer which keywords are best by looking at the keyword data that is provided. By looking at this data, you'll be able to see the most effective keywords in terms of your business goals, not just in terms of visibility.

The data from your analytics program will give you the information you need to improve your SEO results. If you are getting traffic from a keyword, but the conversion rate is low, take a look at the offer on the landing page to see if it's relevant to the keyword that the user is searching on. If not, test another offer to try to improve results. Remember that this may not be the only keyword that is driving traffic to that page, so take care when making offer changes. You may improve the conversion rate on one offer, but lower it on another one.

Another way to use the SEO conversion data is to make changes to your SEO keyword strategy. Instead of guessing about the keywords that you think are going to make a difference for your business, website analytics will tell you which ones are actually working. You can adjust your SEO keyword efforts to build content or create links for keywords that are working so that you can get even better results.

Social Media—Social Media is often criticized for being an unmeasurable marketing activity, much like PR. While some of the value of social media cannot be measured, you can clearly see the impact that social media can have on website traffic and conversions. For example, you can track the number of clicks and goal conversions to your website from major sites like Facebook, YouTube, LinkedIn, and Twitter to see how your content-sharing and fan-building activities are turning into traffic, leads, and sales. This data can help you build a clear return on investment plan for social media and help you justify your budget.

Email—Email campaigns often include many metrics, such as the open rate or click-through rate, that are not visible to a website analytics program. Your website analytics software does not know how many emails have been sent, so it can't calculate these two metrics. It can, however, track the number of clicks and conversions generated by each email blast. By adding a unique tracking code to each link, it can measure the results from each individual email campaign.

Paid Search—Since Google Analytics is integrated with Google AdWords, it's easy to see the important metrics from your AdWords search program in Analytics. The important things to track here are the click-through rates and conversion rates to help you see if your investment in search is driving the return on investment you want.

Other Website Performance Goals

In addition to the other specific campaign metrics I've discussed, there are several other important metrics that you should track to see if your website is performing well.

The first one is overall traffic growth. Whether you are using organic search, paid search, email, PR or social media, you should be growing your overall traffic from month to month. More traffic means more opportunities to sell your products and services. Of course, traffic by itself is meaningless, but it's a great starting place, and it's difficult to accomplish your goals without traffic.

Two other general metrics to look at are average visitors' time-on-site and the bounce rate. The time-on-site is the number of minutes and seconds each user spends when arriving at your site before leaving. If people are spending time on your site, it will tell you that your website content is helpful and engaging.

The bounce rate tells you how frequently people are leaving your site, just after they arrive. If your bounce rate is 25%, then a quarter of the people that come to your website are leaving immediately. If you have not filtered out your own employees from your website traffic, then you may create an artificially high bounce rate because people may have their browser home page set to the company website. If this is the case, every time they open their browser they will create a website "click" and a "bounce." In most website analytics programs, it's possible to filter out your own employees' traffic.

Another challenge with the bounce rate is the source of the traffic. A well-designed home page may have a bounce rate of 30–40%. A well-designed landing page from an online ad may have a bounce rate of

90%, which means that 10% are going deeper or converting to a goal. Both of these metrics are healthy given their traffic source.

When building a high-performance marketing program, it's crucial to have a high-quality analytics tool installed on the website to give you the data you need to make decisions and drive continuous improvement.

A well designed website using modern technology can make it much easier to drive traffic, engagement leads, and sales, and help you get into the marketing Zone. You'll be happier and more confident in your digital marketing if you like the design of your website, it has all of the content your prospects need, and it's producing the results you want.

Part VI
Accelerating your
Digital Marketing Programs

Digital Marketing Programs in the Zone

Astrong digital marketing program will use many campaign elements to drive results. While there are dozens of digital marketing strategies to try, and no shortage of people to sell them to you, programs such as Email, Digital Advertising, Search Engine Optimization (SEO), Marketing Automation, and Social Media are core elements of almost every strong campaign. In this chapter I'll show you a number of techniques you can use, but just remember that these tools are evolving rapidly, and it's very important to stay on top of the latest technology and adapt quickly.

A good way to organize these digital marketing techniques is to envision a marketing funnel. Digital Advertising, Search Engine Optimization, and Email marketing can be great tools to drive new leads into the funnel or to drive sales. The goal of most digital marketing programs is to convert that visitor to a lead or sale with a strong website or excellent content. Once you convert the visitor to a lead or even a customer, you can nurture that relationship with email marketing automation and social media marketing.

Marketing Funnel

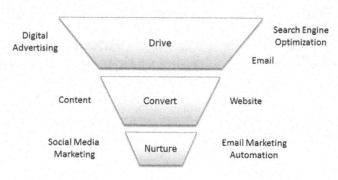

It's easy to just spend money on digital marketing, but when you are in the Zone, you will have a clear understanding of where each campaign element fits, and how it contributes to the success of your marketing campaigns. You will be riding a wave of strong results from each element that gives you the confidence to test new tools and techniques as they become available. An integrated digital marketing program will tie your budget directly to business results, and you will clearly understand the impact you are making on the organization. In addition to a feeling of confidence, you should also experience gratitude from your sales team and senior management for the excellence of your program, which should be very good for your career.

Digital Advertising
in the Zone

Digital Advertising

Digital Advertising is one of the most effective marketing tools ever developed because it is very flexible and lets you target your audience based on their behavior. Many forms of advertising allow you to target your audience based on their demographic characteristics, but search allows you to present an ad when your prospects are actually searching for products like yours. Google, Bing, YouTube, and other search engines use this model to sell advertising in the form of sponsored listings in search engine results.

Google launched AdWords in 2000 based on the idea of presenting relevant ads to people based on the keywords that they are searching on. The idea behind AdWords is that you bid to show your ad when people search on particular keywords. Google will present your ad to searchers based on your keyword bid, the click-through rate (CTR) of your ad, and the quality score Google assigns to your ad. This system allows Google to keep advertisers striving to increase their bids against each other, while improving the quality of their ad copy and offers. This system works so well that advertisers spent over $67 billion in 2015 with Google, up from only $6 billion 10 years ago [10].

Caleb's Digital Advertising Experience

Caleb was the Director of Marketing for a large, membership-driven nonprofit and had a lot on his plate. He was responsible for advertising, PR, and external awareness, and had many members constantly giving him their opinions on the best way to run marketing. The board wanted to grow, and in one year they doubled his ad budget to give him more resources to drive leads for new members.

Caleb had been spending money on Google AdWords, but he was only tracking spending and clicks, so he never knew how many leads were being generated by his campaigns. And he was letting Google decide where to show his ads across the world.

When we started working with Caleb, our first step was to implement better analytics and conversion tracking to get good data on the effectiveness of each campaign. Caleb was surprised when he learned that his cost per conversion was over $200 per lead. Instead of the data inspiring confidence, he was suddenly scared of wasting the organization's money on a campaign that was not effective. He also learned that half of his ad spending was in India, which represented only a small part of his target market.

Our next step was to redesign the landing pages to feature an information kit, which potential members could download. We

---

10   Source: Statista. Footnote at www.marketing-in-the-zone.com/footnotes

also reallocated the budget rationally across all regions of the world to get consistent lead flow for all regions.

The result of the campaign was a dramatic increase in lead flow across the globe. Caleb moved from confusion to confidence that he could increase the ad budget and get strong results. When he finally increased the budget and also introduced Facebook Advertising, the cost per lead dropped below $30, which meant that he was getting six times the lead flow for each dollar invested. The new campaign was a total success and the board was so confident that they increased the ad budget again the following year.

Digital Advertising Strategy

Digital advertising enables you to present your ads and optimize your budget to reach your target market in the most efficient way possible. You can target specific keywords or phrases by focusing your ads on Google's search page, their partner search pages, or thousands of other sites that show Google ads. You can also target based on geography, language, and a variety of other demographic characteristics.

Traditional marketing techniques target users based on demographics alone. If you are interested in reaching a certain demographic, say, upper income women between 30 and 40, you could choose various radio, TV, website, or magazine options. These advertising platforms typically run surveys to find out how much of their audience falls in to each demographic.

The challenge with these media is that the users are generally doing something else when they are viewing your ad, such as reading an article or watching a TV program, so the response rates are often low. In addition, even though these media are targeted, they always have some users that fall outside of the demographic you want to reach.

This traditional media is often referred to as "push" or "outbound" marketing, since you are pushing your message in front of an audience that may or may not be interested. For example, if you work for a college recruiting students and you advertise in a magazine or website focused on young women, you are presenting your ads to the right audience, but presenting the ad at a time when they are reading about fashion or some other topic.

When people are searching on Google, they are actively looking for something. If an ad helps answer their question, then it's natural for them to respond to the ad to learn more. The power of Google AdWords is that you are presenting your ad to searchers the moment they type a query. This makes your ad not only much more relevant, but very timely. You can also fulfill the searcher's need immediately with more information faster than you could with any print or traditional media. This is known as "pull" or "inbound" marketing, as you are pulling in an audience that has—through their Google search—expressed an interest in your offering.

Targeting ads based on what people are thinking about and actually searching for is very powerful and can result in a cost per lead or cost per sale that is lower than almost any other type of paid media. The key to making the program work is to align all of the variables available to you in order to achieve your business goals. The main variables available to the advertiser are:

- Keywords
- Ad Copy
- Display Ad Design and Copy
- Offers
- Landing Page Design
- Bids
- Budget

- Geographic Targeting
- Website Targeting

The power of the system is that you can run multiple ads featuring multiple offers on thousands of keywords at the same time and make instant changes to improve your results. These campaigns can be created and taken down very rapidly, and you can start very small and later grow them very large.

In each of these categories, you can also create and test many options to give you the best results. For example, a campaign may contain 500 keyword variations grouped into ten ad groups, testing 35 text ads and eight banner (graphical) ads, that leverage five offers supported by dozens of very specific landing pages, showing ads in 16 countries across three continents. All of this can be managed through one user interface where changes can be made very quickly and easily.

The flexibility of the system serves the needs of large international advertisers, very small local advertisers, and everyone in between. Compared to any traditional media, it is easier to get started, less expensive to run and manage, easier to get fast results, and more conducive to testing and optimizing.

Because there are many variables that you can arrange in order to make a campaign work, I've sometimes heard people say that they tried Google AdWords, but it didn't work for them. Although it does not always work, most of the time the reason it does not work is because people use these tools poorly and do not tailor all of the variables properly to produce the desired results.

Creating an Effective Search Advertising Campaign

An effective campaign has a clear strategy, highly targeted channels and keywords, a strong offer or series of offers, and well-designed landing pages. It is also managed continually through testing, targeting, and optimization.

Goals for a Google AdWords Campaign

Several of the goals I've seen used for a Google campaign are:

- **Brand Impressions.** Some companies simply want to be seen. Since Google presents your ad for free and only charges you when someone clicks on it, it can be very inexpensive to create ad impressions. In one of our campaigns we got over 1 million impressions for less than $1,000.
- **Clicks to your website.** Since Google is a pay-per-click system, they charge you based on the number of clicks you get to your website or landing page. This can be a great way to generate traffic to your site at an attractive cost per click.
- **Conversions.** Most companies don't simply want impressions; they want leads or a sale, usually referred to as a "conversion." The power of AdWords is that if you align all of the variables properly, you can optimize the program to drive the most conversions at the lowest cost/conversion.
- **Sales.** If you run an e-commerce website, it's very easy to see how the money you are investing in search can turn directly into revenue. If you are a B2B marketer, you are often driving leads that don't turn into sales instantly. Google AdWords integrates with popular CRM systems such as Salesforce.com, which allows you to track a sale back to the keyword or ad that

drove the lead, even if the sale was made months or years after it was first generated.

The beauty of an AdWords program is that you can focus part of your campaign on one goal and another part of your campaign on another goal. For example, you may want to make sure your company or a product name is at the top of the search results page to make your brand more visible. You can put your brand keywords in a campaign with a specific budget, and get the most impressions possible without disrupting your core lead generation campaigns. You can do the same thing with your other goals, creating specific budgeted campaigns to serve your website traffic, sales, or lead generation goals.

The Offer

Many companies violate a basic principle of direct marketing and use AdWords to direct traffic to their website home page. The offer in their ad is often something to the effect of, "We're great—check us out." In test after test, we've discovered that ads are more effective when there is a strong offer and a specific call to action. Instead of just saying that you are great, it's more effective to offer 20% off a purchase or a free eBook. These types of valuable offers deliver value to the user and drive higher click-through rates than other, more self-focused ads.

The power of AdWords, of course, is that you don't need to use just one offer. You can feature a different offer for every keyword group to make the offers more and more relevant. We've run campaigns with dozens of different offers to meet the needs of users who are searching on different keywords. The more relevant the offer is to the keyword you are advertising on, the higher your click-through rate and conversion rate.

Landing Pages

Once you have your offer strategy developed, you can create landing pages. Landing pages help you avoid the mistake of taking your AdWords traffic directly back to your home page, which may not be relevant to the searcher on every keyword that you are advertising on. Additionally, your home page offers many navigation choices, and if your goal is to drive leads or a sale, the user will be distracted by all of these choices and less likely to do what you want them to do.

A landing page fulfills the goal of the searcher. When someone searches on a keyword and clicks on a specific ad, they expect to go to a place that fulfills their needs. If they don't see it within seconds, they will hit the back button and continue searching.

A well-designed landing page makes it easy for the user to get what they want, while allowing you to get what you want. If your goal is to drive leads, then you want to make it easy for them to give you their contact information with a simple form that's easily visible when they arrive on the page. You'll also want to make it easy for the user to understand the offer by providing a clear headline with short copy and a picture of the offer. The call to action should be clear and simple so that the user can give you their contact information within seconds.

Good landing pages can make a significant impact on a campaign. I've seen a 500% improvement in results by creating a dedicated landing page instead of using the home page. I've also seen a massive improvement in results by creating a well-designed landing page instead of a rambling, multi-page website. These improvements in conversion rates can create a dramatic improvement in the ROI of a campaign.

Targeting and Optimization

Once you create an AdWords campaign with well-designed offers, landing pages, keywords, and ad groups, your work has just begun.

The AdWords marketplace is always changing with companies constantly competing on keyword bids in a live auction environment. There is a large, but finite number of searches by individuals happening every day, so it's important to review the campaign daily and make adjustments based on what the marketplace is telling you.

Because of this dynamic environment, campaign results can change rapidly when your competitors adjust their budgets, bids, or keywords. It's very important to constantly monitor your campaigns to make sure that the elements that were working last week are still working this week.

Key Performance Indicators (KPI)

AdWords campaigns can produce a lot of data, but it's important to monitor the most important variables to keep a campaign in line. When we manage a B2B campaign, for example, the most important variables we focus on are the campaign budget, the number of conversions (leads), and the cost per conversion. In other words, are we spending enough money, driving enough leads or sales, and doing it at an acceptable cost per lead? If we achieve these goals, the rest of the campaign will be in line. It's important to review this data at the account level, and also at the campaign, ad group, or even keyword level. This way you can determine the effectiveness of each of your campaigns.

By using the principles I've outlined here and creating consistent and predictable results, you can accelerate your search marketing results. You will move into the Zone when you feel confident that you've created an excellent program and engaged your target audience with the best ads, offers, and landing pages, and you have the results to prove it.

Social Media Advertising in the Zone

Social Media Advertising

Social media advertising is an important and fast-growing part of digital advertising. In this chapter, I'll present social media advertising trends, show why they are important, and then help you understand how to use social media advertising in your business.

In addition, I'll show you how to integrate your organic or natural social media marketing program with your paid social media advertising program. I'll also show you specifically how to use Facebook, LinkedIn, and Twitter campaign targeting, and give you a few tips that should help you be more effective with using targeting to get exactly the audience and the results you want.

What is social media advertising? As simple as it sounds, it's really just advertising on social media sites. The advantage of social media advertising over other forms of digital advertising is that social media sites get a lot of traffic, and they have a lot of demographic information on their users, and you can use this data to target your ads very effectively.

Sharon's Social Media Advertising Program

Sharon was responsible for Social Media Marketing at a large tech company. She had a strong team creating and posting content on a variety of social media properties including Facebook, LinkedIn, and Twitter.

While she had a fairly good base of followers, she wanted more engagement with her content from people in her target market. She was doing the hard work of creating content, but she was frustrated that not enough people were actually reading and engaging with it.

To get more engagement, we created a comprehensive and highly targeted social media advertising program. We used the targeting tools available in the major social media sites to identify the people in her target audience and featured the right posts to get their attention. Some of the ads were ongoing, and others were targeted around specific events and conferences to get even more leverage from these programs. The result of the campaign was a significant increase in engagement with her content.

Sharon moved from a feeling of frustration to confidence that she was able to leverage paid social media advertising to get solid results from people in her target audience.

Why Social Media Advertising?

Social media advertising is big, and it's getting bigger. There are literally billions of people who are engaged with social media today, with over 1.7 billion users on Facebook, and a billion users on YouTube.

There are also hundreds of millions of people on LinkedIn, Twitter, Instagram, and Google Plus. When I first started talking about social media advertising and social media marketing with my clients a few years ago, they often said, "I wonder if my customers are using Facebook?" or "I wonder if they're on Twitter or LinkedIn?"

Today, that's not even a question. If you are still wondering if your customers or your prospects are using social media, you don't have to wonder anymore. They are using it!

The Growth of Facebook

Facebook has seen tremendous growth over the last few years and is now a part of the fabric of our daily lives. Because of this growth, Facebook is taking a huge share of total Internet traffic.

Social media sites such as Facebook, Instagram, LinkedIn, and Twitter should be a part of your marketing mix so that you can reach your target audience and build an overall strategy for success. By using a mix of different digital advertising tools, you can easily shift your budget into what's most effective and working best for your campaigns.

Growth in Social Media Advertising

Because of this new way of reaching specific groups of people and interacting with people through engagement and likes, social media is growing very rapidly. In 2016, over $14 billion was spent on social media advertising, and that is projected to grow to almost $25 billion by 2021[11]. We're going to continue to see a strong increase in social ad budgets over the next few years as advertisers realize more of the benefits of social media advertising.

Although social media advertising is growing, seventy percent of advertisers are allocating 10% or less of their budget to social media

---

11   Source: Statista. Footnote at www.marketing-in-the-zone.com/footnotes

advertising, and only thirteen percent have 20% or more of their budget allocated in this area.

While Google's market share has been very steady over the last few years with about 61% of digital worldwide ad revenue, Facebook has gone from 4% to almost 8% over the last two years. That's amazing growth in a very short period of time because of its wide reach, advanced targeting, and multiple engagement techniques.

Among the social media sites, Facebook has the most users, and it's also getting the most advertising market share. Facebook gets about 57% of the average social media ad budget compared to smaller budgets for some of the others because it has the most people, great targeting options, and a lot of traffic, with an average of 655 million daily users.

Paid Advertising vs. Organic Social Media Marketing

How does this advertising strategy fit in with what you're doing in social media? In a typical organic social media program, you need to do at least three things. First, you create a solid presence on LinkedIn, Twitter, Instagram, Facebook, Pinterest, etc., making these platforms look great, making them look powerful, and making them look professional. I'll describe this in more detail in the chapter on social media marketing.

Once you have the platforms built, you need to fill them with content that might include Tweets, posts, and video. To make this work well, you need to create and send content about your company and products, as well as industry content so that your presence looks interesting and engaging.

While you are sending out content, you also need to build your follower base. In an organic social media program, having great platforms and pushing out content is meaningless if nobody's listening to you, so it's important to build your follower base so that you can generate business results. As you build followers and send out posts, you can integrate offers with a call to action. The outcome should be that you get more likes, more traffic, more leads, and more sales.

Here's an example of how this works in a typical organic social media program: If you have a few hundred followers and you're doing 20 posts a month, this could result in 10,000 potential brand impressions per month. If you had 10,000 followers with 200 posts a month, there could be 2 million potential brand impressions each month. This all can lead to likes, traffic, leads, and sales for your business. In practice, the number of brand impressions will be much lower, because people don't read all of the social media content that is directed toward them, but it can still drive traffic and engagement.

How does advertising fit into this? Instead of doing all of the work to build your followers and push out a lot of content, you can just pay to promote your posts. Paid ads can take out all of the work of building followers and you can still get the same or even better results.

Paid social media advertising is a way to complement what you're doing through organic social media. By leveraging the posts and content that you're already pushing out with your organic program, you can get traffic and engagement when you might not have enough followers or the volume of content you need in your organic program. These two parts of your social media program can work well together.

One of the interesting things about social media is that you can use it for more than just direct response or brand building. Social media enables you to build and measure engagement by getting people to like you, follow you, comment, or even share your content.

With engagement metrics, you can measure the number of views that you get on social media, how many times people comment on something you're talking about, and how many times they share what you're saying.

You can also use social media to get more likes and followers for your organic social media program. Getting likes and followers is almost like getting someone to sign up for your email list because they're volunteering to get more information from you.

Unlike an email channel, where you might send them an email a month or an email a week, in social media, you can push out content to them one to five times per day. Your followers are giving you permission to send a lot of content.

Facebook Targeting

Facebook is a powerful advertising platform because of its reach and its ability to direct your ads to a very specific target audience. While there are hundreds of targeting options, three targeting options—age, country, and interest are used by most Facebook advertisers.

Facebook gives you a lot of other targeting options because they know so much about their users. You can advertise and target by types of interests and you can be very specific about the kinds of interest categories that you want.

For example, if you are promoting a Chinese restaurant, you could choose the restaurant category, and then you can target people who are specifically interested in Chinese restaurants. As you select different demographic or interest categories, you can see your audience numbers change. This enables you to control the size of your audience—not too small or too big—and make sure that it fits your ad budget and your business objectives.

Facebook also provides conversion tracking in their ad platform to track the results of your advertising. By placing a conversion-tracking code on your website thank you pages, you can measure and track your conversions. Some of the options that you can choose are sales checkouts, registrations, leads, key page views, adds to shopping cart, or other website conversions. This tool lets you measure results for exactly the kind of conversions that you're trying to get for your campaign.

Comparing Facebook to Google AdWords

If you have been using Google AdWords, you're probably wondering how it compares to Facebook advertising. In Google AdWords, people are searching, and your ads are a response to those queries. In Facebook advertising, your ad shows up in the user's content stream even when they are not searching for your product.

In AdWords, you filter users by keyword, and it allows you to design campaigns with positive and negative keywords along with many other targeting options. In Facebook, you're targeting based on user demographics and interests. In Google, your options are to get people to click on an ad and then send them down a conversion pathway. In Facebook, you get the option of starting a long-term relationship with someone by getting them to like you or to engage with you or to comment on your content.

In Google, you can use several ad types such as text ads, product listing ads, or banner ads. You can use geo-targeting, language targeting, and other demographic targeting variables. As I mentioned earlier, you have a lot more targeting options within Facebook.

In AdWords, Google assigns a quality score to your ads based on historical data, which determines your cost per click and ultimately your cost per conversion or cost per sale. Facebook determines quality based on user feedback, and Facebook tracks the user's response rate, which will ultimately determine how your ads are displayed.

Google AdWords is a cost-per-click (CPC) media, while in Facebook, you can use either CPC or cost per thousand, which gives you more flexibility. Campaigns in Google AdWords and Facebook can both be effective, but there are some significant differences in how they work.

LinkedIn

If you've got a B2B product or service, LinkedIn (now owned by Microsoft) can also be very effective for you. LinkedIn has about 300 million members today, and 12 million small businesses. They know a lot about their users, such as name, position, company, and location. They know the groups we're part of and the things we post and share, as well as our interests. LinkedIn offers advertisers a lot of different targeting variables that are unique to their network.

With LinkedIn advertising, you can do geographic targeting and targeting by company. You can even target your ads to a specific company, so that you can reach out specifically to people who work for General Electric, IBM, or Microsoft, for example.

You can also target people by type of company, industry, or size of company. You can also target people by job function or seniority. Seniority targeting here is another very powerful option, for example, if you only want to reach senior executives.

LinkedIn also offers other targeting options because many people use it to store their resumes and other personal information. This gives you the ability to target people by school or by job skill. You can also target by group so that you can get a very focused audience for your ads.

Twitter Advertising

Twitter, as you saw from the statistics I shared earlier, is a smaller player in digital advertising, but it's coming on strong, and its market share has tripled in the last few years.

In Twitter advertising, you are promoting Tweets, and these are the same Tweets you post in your organic campaign. You can target by location, by category, and by users with the same interests, and you can get very specific within your campaign.

You can target by interest, and also target users with the same interests as other followers, which is a great way to find people that have the same interests as people that are already following you. As you build your target audience, you can see how large your audience is.

You can use advertising to promote all kinds of Tweets. You can promote Tweets with a call to action. You can promote Tweets that go back to your website. You can build your budget around the number of impressions or the number of clicks that you want from your campaign. You can also control all the different bidding options, your budget per day, as well as your budget per engagement.

Accelerating your Social Media Marketing Program

Why advertise on social media? First, there is a huge audience, literally billions of people, so if you're selling any kind of a product or service, you will find an audience on Facebook, Twitter, and LinkedIn. There's also very strong momentum, and your fellow marketers are using these tools in greater and greater numbers.

Social Media advertising also gives you advanced targeting options that allow you to use many targeting tools to match your ad to your target audience. Facebook also gives you multiple engagement and conversion options to make it easier to match your advertising program to your business goals.

You can generate engagement. You can generate views. You can generate comments. You can generate likes and followers, as well as traffic leads and sales, and you can measure all of it.

You can also focus on mobile users. More and more of us are using our mobile devices to access content on the Internet, and today about 70% of Facebook users are mobile, so it's a great way to engage with the mobile user.

Perhaps the most important business reason to use social media advertising is that you may experience a lower cost per click and lower cost per conversion compared to other types of digital advertising campaigns.

For all of these reasons, it makes sense to leverage social media as part of an integrated, optimized advertising campaign because it can be very effective.

When you've implemented a strong social media marketing program, you will be confident that you are reaching the target audience that is best for your products and services. You will see consistent and strong results and intuitively be able to test new social media sites and use them successfully.

Search Engine Optimization in the Zone

SEO Strategy

O n any given day, Google services 3.5 billion searches, or 40,000 searches per second[12]. Google and Bing are in the business of indexing all of the content they can, and making relevant content available to people as they search. Once people find what they are looking for, they naturally click to learn more, and this generates a massive amount of traffic to websites all over the world.

The search engines provide this as a free service for both the searcher and the website, because they make a tremendous amount of money on paid ads. We call the free search results "organic" or "natural" search, since they are a natural result of the search engine's work and not influenced by paid advertising.

---

12   Source: Internet Live Stats. Footnote at www.marketing-in-the-zone.com/footnotes

Search Engine Optimization (SEO) is the art and science of making your website look like what the search engines want to see for a particular keyword so that you show up as high as possible in the organic search engine rankings. The important thing to note is that it's not about tricking the search engines into thinking you are more relevant than you really are; it's about making your website as relevant as possible based on their criteria.

Since the search engines don't actually publish their search algorithms, it's only possible to understand how to make your website more relevant by trial and error. Fortunately, there is an entire industry of SEO specialists who focus on this problem every day, so after years of study, we have a very clear understanding of what works and what does not.

Here are the steps you should take to create an effective SEO program.

SEO Strategy → SEO Technical Website Optimization → SEO Website Content Optimization → Link Building with Content

Ann's SEO Program

Ann was the CEO of a software company and she needed leads for her growing sales team. When I first met her, she told me about a problem with her organic website search traffic. She had just implemented a new website, and the firm that designed and developed it did not handle the SEO transition well, so after the new site went live, her organic search traffic and visibility dropped to almost nothing. This also caused a dramatic drop in lead flow, and the sales team was screaming for leads.

We got involved and worked closely with Ann and her team to SEO optimize all of the pages and tags on their website and blog so that they were consistent and relevant to Google. We also created articles and built links back to her website from other sites, including social media sites.

After one year, organic search visibility went from 50 keywords on the first page to 700 keywords on the first page and organic search traffic increased by 400%.

Ann was not satisfied with just increasing traffic, she also wanted leads, so we worked with her to feature the best white paper offers on the home page and to increase the conversion rate of the website so that the total lead flow increased dramatically.

The leads turned into sales, and Ann was able to complete a successful company merger with a larger company in order to get the funding she needed to continue to grow the business. Ann moved from frustration to confidence because she was getting better keyword visibility, traffic, and leads to make her business succeed.

SEO Goals

When you get started on an SEO program, the first thing to do is to consider is your goals. Are you interested in the visibility of certain keywords for their own sake, better branding, sales, or more leads?

Whatever your goals, make sure that you focus on them and then track the results of your activity. Most of our clients consider SEO to be an important tool to help them become more visible in the search engines in order to generate more traffic to their website, which in turn creates fresh leads or sales.

Remember that in order for the new business to happen, your website needs to be set up to catch and convert the traffic, which will require a good design, sound architecture, and a strong call to action.

All keywords, of course, are not created equal. It will be much easier to rank #1 on your company name than for a keyword like "financial services." Not only do more general keywords have more traffic, they are also much more competitive, which makes it more challenging to rank well on general terms. If you are successful getting on the first page of a keyword with high traffic, it can make a big difference for your business. If you are successful in being visible on a keyword with little or no traffic, you might not even notice.

Remember that your end goal is not just visibility, but traffic and ultimately sales or leads, so choose your keywords carefully. If you end up ranking on a keyword that is not relevant to your business, you may increase traffic to your website, but you may also increase the bounce rate from your website, since people clicking to your website from that keyword will leave seconds after they arrive.

Traffic, of course, is a result of clicks to your website, not just being visible on a search. Once you search for something, you'll naturally read the search results to find the content that is most relevant for you. This means that you'll need to work on the copy that Google shows as part of the search result to make it enticing for the user so that you'll actually get a click.

Most of the time, the search engine will get this copy from the meta description tag content in your HTML page, so take care to write the copy so that you'll encourage the reader to not only see it, but also to click.

Then look at the page you link to in order to make sure that there is an offer there that is relevant to the searcher. Only if you connect all of the dots will you be able to make sure you've done all that you can to turn your visibility into clicks and ultimately leads or sales.

What's Important to Google

There are really only two things that matter to Google that will determine how you rank on the search engine's organic results. This is their "special sauce" and the reason they dominate the search market and are worth about $546 billion[13]. These two things are "on page" factors and inbound links.

On page factors are things about your site that tell Google that you are relevant for a particular keyword. These are keywords in the body copy, URLs, other HTML tags, and the quality of your domain.

Inbound links are totally different and much harder to control. These are typically links from other websites to specific pages on your website. Linking is essentially a popularity contest where Google gives credit for the most popular pages as determined by the links.

Do other websites link to your site with keywords that are relevant? Are these important websites? It makes a big difference if CNN or IBM link to your website vs. getting a link from a non-relevant site with very little traffic.

Keyword Research

You should begin your SEO program by determining the most effective keywords for placement on your website—words that have low competition and high traffic, and that are highly relevant to your business. It's advisable to start with dozens or even hundreds of potential keywords and then get data on keyword traffic and competition in order to make decisions about the best keywords to focus on.

You can also get data from your website analytics program or a paid search marketing program to see which keywords are not only driving traffic, but are also driving leads or sales. You can also see which keywords you are already ranking on, and focus on improving existing organic search term visibility.

For example, if you are showing up on the middle of the second page for a particular keyword, it will be much easier to improve visibility

---

13   Source: Alphabet Market Cap as of August 2016. Footnote at www.marketing-in-the-zone.com/footnotes

and get on the first page than to take a keyword on which you are not ranking at all, and become visible.

It's challenging to make decisions about the best keywords to use with all of this data, but since these decisions will drive the success of the rest of the program, it's critical to do it well.

A Keyword Plan for your Website

Once you've chosen your keywords, you'll need to develop a plan to build them into your website. In this process, you will need to insert the keywords into the HTML and body copy of the page. The common HTML tags to focus on are the URL, the title tag, description tag, alt tag, H1 tag, and body copy.

It's important to insert the keywords enough times to make the content seem relevant, but not enough times to seem to be "spamming" the search engines. If Google decides that you are trying to trick them, they could blacklist you so that you don't show up at all on the search engines.

One way to see how many times to insert the keyword into each tag is to look at the top organic results for that keyword and see how long their copy is for each tag and how many times they've used the keyword in each tag. This will give you a sense of what the search engines think is important for each keyword.

If this sounds like a very detailed process, you are right. To do this well, you need to match at least one web page to every keyword you are focused on, and then write copy for all of the different tags mentioned above that include the keyword. This SEO copywriting and HTML implementation can take time, but it is a critical step in the process of making your website more visible to the search engines.

Website SEO Analysis

Once you've built keywords into your website, you'll want the search engines to index the content and update your website in their search engine rankings. Google has a very helpful tool called Google Search Console, which allows you see your website the way that the search engines do. It will help you identify broken links or other factors that may be preventing them from seeing all of your web pages.

You can also tell the search engines not to index certain content on your website if you don't want them to see it. These would be pages like landing pages or ads, which have duplicate content or even pages you, don't want searchers to see.

Fresh Content

Fresh content is a very important factor in keyword visibility. If your site is updated frequently, the search engines will index it more frequently and it will help you get better keyword visibility.

A regularly updated blog is an excellent way to provide fresh content. It can also be helpful to make small updates to your product or service pages each month.

Press releases on your site are another easy way to make your content fresh. As you add new content, make sure you use all of the same principles mentioned above to make sure that the new HTML page body copy as well as the tags and links are fully optimized.

Link Building

As I mentioned at the beginning of this discussion on SEO, inbound links are a very important part of the search engines' algorithm, which determines how your keywords will rank in the organic search results. Each link is essentially a vote for your site's content. The more votes your site has, the more popular you'll be in search engine results.

It is very important, therefore, to get as many high-quality inbound links as possible pointing to the most important pages of your website. When you build links, make sure that you use keyword-seeded anchor text across multiple websites to increase your inbound links. You can get links by signing up with directories, issuing press releases, getting partners to link to you, linking from your own microsites, and posting on social media sites.

There is an almost limitless number of ways for you to get links, but all of them take time and effort. As you build links, keep track of how Google views your link-building progress through Google Search Console to make sure you are focused on getting links that will make a difference.

Don't forget to include internal links to your most important pages to help search engine spiders easily identify which pages they should pay closer attention to. Visitors will also benefit from internal linking since you'll be promoting related or more in-depth information on a given topic. And don't forget to optimize your anchor text on these internal links as well.

SEO Reporting and Analytics

After you set up your goals, SEO optimize the content and tags on your website, and build all of the internal and external links you can, you'll want to know what parts of the program are working and what still needs improvement. And you'll need a way to quantify the business impact of your SEO work.

To get a good understanding of the effectiveness of your SEO program, you'll need to understand how your keyword visibility has changed over time, how much traffic that visibility is driving to the website, and what is happening to that traffic.

There are many tools that will give you data on keyword visibility. Tools such as HubSpot, MOZ, Keyword Spy, or SEM Rush can quickly tell you how visible your keywords are. If you keep track of your results from month to month, you'll be able to see the impact of your work on visibility over time.

Keyword visibility, of course, is only the first step in the process. What you really want to know is how your visibility is impacting traffic and leads or sales. To get this data, you'll need to use a website analytics program like Google Analytics.

This tool will tell you how much traffic and how many goal conversions you get from each keyword. By tying your visibility to traffic to conversions, you can get a complete picture of the business impact of your SEO work.

SEO Summary

Search engine optimization should be treated as a living and breathing organism—it needs constant attention in order to be truly successful. By conducting ongoing analysis and identifying new and inventive ways to continuously improve your search engine visibility, you'll be in the Zone and a step ahead of the competition.

Email Marketing in the Zone

According to the Direct Marketing Association, email marketing delivers the highest ROI of any marketing program with a return of 21–23% for every dollar invested[14]. That's an amazing return. Imagine if your bank gave you an interest rate of 22% for every dollar you invested with them. How much would you invest? As much as you possibly can! The big caveat here is that you need to do email marketing well in order to get this ROI. In practice, an email campaign is limited by the size and quality of your email list, and because of this, you should use the strategies here to get the most out of every campaign.

An effective email marketer is great at building the audience, creating fantastic emails, getting the emails delivered, achieving high open rates, creating calls-to-action that work, and optimizing campaign metrics.

14　Source: Marketing Charts. Footnote at www.marketing-in-the-zone.com/footnotes

When you do all of this well, people respond and your email campaign works. If you don't do all of this well, it can be very quiet after you hit "send," and it might seem like tens of thousands or millions of your emails went into a big void.

Lisa's Email Marketing Program

Lisa worked for a mid-sized consumer products company that made gift candles, and she wanted to improve communications with the hundreds of retailers that carried their products in order to drive more sales. These retailers were often small shops and the candle section was frequently a small, but very profitable, part of their business.

Email was a natural way to reach out to the retailers to communicate specials and new seasonal products that they could purchase for their stores. When we started working with Lisa she was sending a simple text email that got a poor response rate.

We started by designing a clean and clear email template that highlighted the firm's branding, and also allowed us to customize the email with new products and specials each month. We also started using a high-quality email service provider to improve deliverability, track opt-outs, and maintain legal SPAM compliance. The results of these changes were amazing. The emails got an open rate of 40%, which is over twice the industry average, and sales increased because retailers were ordering better product.

This email campaign made an immediate impact on the business and Lisa felt more confident and secure in the relationships her company had with their retailers. She moved from confusion and anxiety to the Zone.

Email Strategy

To create a high-performance email program, it's very important to focus on email campaign optimization techniques that will get more of your emails delivered, opened, and acted upon. When developing an email campaign, the most critical elements you can use to achieve these goals are using a good list, featuring a strong offer, and presenting a powerful creative.

Once you have your email strategy in place, it's important to execute the campaign well by using a high-quality email tool and paying close attention to all of the details that make a program work, such as lowering your SPAM score to improve your deliverability.

As you send your email, you should test different elements of the campaign, such as the subject line, in order to improve your results. To make your email program even more effective, you can also integrate it with other online marketing activities such as search and social media marketing.

A high-performance email program will use the strongest email tools and best practices available to deliver the best results possible. By using the techniques described here, you'll no longer be satisfied with just getting higher open rates and lower opt-out rates. You'll be focused on getting more leads and sales, and with every email sent you'll be learning more and more about what drives results.

Here are the steps you'll need to take create a powerful email program:

Email Marketing Goals

When you start an email marketing campaign, it's critical to have clear goals in mind. Do you want to simply inform your audience? Do you want them to click to your website to read content? Do you want them to watch a video, download a trial, or even buy something?

Your goals for the campaign will directly influence the design, frequency, and messaging of the email program. It will also determine the reporting metrics you put in place during the campaign set up process to help you see if you are accomplishing your goals.

The Email Audience

It's critical to clearly understand your audience when you begin your email program. Several different groups you may consider creating email programs for are:

- Your top customers
- All existing customers
- Partners
- Potential customers who have opted in to get information from you
- Other potential customers in your target market

You should plan to communicate with each of these groups using email in a different way. Your best customers may receive a personalized email from the CEO and be invited to special events or to provide product or service feedback.

All existing customers may receive a regular email newsletter with updates on the company, products and services, or other important announcements. They may also receive emails with special offers to encourage them to buy other products or services from you.

Partners may be interested in some of the same content as your best customers, but you need to speak to them as part of the team, not as potential buyers. A partner email newsletter can be an effective tool for this audience.

Potential customers who have "raised their hand" and opted in to receive your content may receive a stream of content designed to move them through the buying process. If this is a B2B audience, this content may include offers for white papers, webinars, demos, case studies, product information, or the opportunity to evaluate the product. A B2C audience may get special offers, discounts, or advance notice on promotions.

While some companies only send email to existing customers and people who have opted in, many organizations send email to potential customers. These emails may be highly promotional with strong offers that encourage the user to opt in to get deeper content.

It's important to design an email campaign strategy that takes the specific needs of different audience types into account and then communicates to them in a personalized way based on their relationship with the company.

Email List

A strong email list is critical to any email campaign. When I say a "strong" list, what I really mean is one that is large, highly targeted, and with complete data. I've been involved in several campaigns where the client invests a lot of time, energy, and money into developing a beautiful email creative, but then only sends it to a few hundred people because they do not have a good list. This is obviously a waste of time and effort since it costs very little to extend a good campaign to a larger email list.

When you do the math, you can see why this can be a problem. If you spend $5,000 developing an email campaign (offer, email creative, landing page, etc.) and then send it to only 500 people, you may only get 5 people to respond if you get a 1% response rate.

Your cost in this case is a whopping $1,000/lead. If you have a list of 100,000 people, and you get a 1% response rate, you can yield 1,000 leads and drop your cost to $5 per lead. That's a very powerful change in the effectiveness of the campaign, simply by leveraging the email campaign across a larger audience.

In a perfect world, your list should include everyone in your target audience. Yes, everyone! Your list database should also include information beyond their email address, such as whether or not they've opted in to receive your content, and their relationship to your company (customer, partner, potential customer, etc.). This will allow you to do some basic targeting.

Ideally, it should also have other data that will allow you to segment emails to them more effectively. This may include their name, company, location, industry, past purchases, how frequently they'd like to hear from you, preferences, and other variables that will allow you to personalize and customize your email.

Most organizations do not have anywhere close to this type of list, but if you do, it's a powerful competitive advantage, since you can easily and inexpensively reach your target market.

You can build your list by collecting email addresses from trusted sources. First, make sure you get the emails of your existing customers and partners. Since these are your best contacts, it's worth the time to contact them directly to make sure the information is accurate and complete. If you have offers and landing pages on your website, inbound leads can also be an effective source. If you have a sales team, they can also be a significant source of email addresses if they are using a CRM system to manage customer and prospect data. Your partners can also be a source of emails if they are willing to share them with you.

It can take a long time to build your list using the techniques above, so you may be tempted to buy a list to get faster results. There are many places where you can buy a list, but be careful. Even the best lists I've purchased have a significant number of bad email addresses.

If you buy a list, make sure you only send emails to small batches of the list over a long period of time so that you can manage the opt-outs properly and don't get tagged as a spammer and blacklisted by the Internet Service Providers.

Once you have a list, it's very important to keep it clean and up-to-date. In some markets, 10% of the people change jobs or their email address every year and need to be removed from the list. Also, people will opt out from receiving your emails and will need to be removed from your list.

People will also change their relationship with your company and their records will need to be updated when they move from prospect to customer, or from customer to "important customer" so you can send appropriate messages to them.

From time to time, you may also want to remove people from the list who do not respond to your email programs at all. These non-responders lower your response rates and may cost you money to mail to. Continuing to send mail to inactive records over time can also get you labeled as a spammer and lower the response rates of your entire campaign. Rather than deleting these records, you may want to break them out into a different segment for occasional important promotions to see if you can reengage them with strong offers.

Once you have built a strong list, it will become a powerful asset for your company and must be protected and managed to keep it working effectively.

The Offer

Email campaigns should be designed around an offer. The offer is something special that you are giving to your audience in order to get them to respond. The offer should be strong enough that it gets people to open the email, read it, click through, and take the action you want them to take. The stronger and more relevant the offer, the better the response rate for the campaign.

When you are designing an email campaign, it is often helpful to think about how you react to receiving emails yourself. If you get an email that features an update on a company's executive team, you're less likely to respond than if you get one that features a free industry analyst paper, free software, a coupon, or the chance to win a valuable prize. Always try to put yourself in the shoes of the recipient when you design your offer strategy, and feature the strongest offer you can in each email campaign.

Email Creative Design

Although the design of the email won't make as much difference to the success of the campaign as the list and the offer do, it's still very important to design an email that represents your brand well, clearly communicates your message and offer, and makes it easy to respond.

The best emails feature a clean, compelling design and engaging copy. The email should not be too long and easy to read, since people read emails very quickly to see whether or not they contain something of value for them.

The copy should be engaging and short, and it should be very easy to see the call to action or what to do next. As you write the copy for the email, make sure you include compelling headlines, strong copy, and a clear call to action to motivate people to take the action you want.

As you design the email, pay special attention to the call to action. If you want the user to do something, design it so that the action stands out with a special color or other design treatment to make it easy for them to see what to do.

It's also critical to put the action above the fold at the top of the email so that the user does not need to scroll down in order to take the next step. You may also consider putting the call to action in multiple places, such as a button on the top right of the email and a text link within the body copy in case the recipient has images disabled.

A critical part of any email is the subject line. This is the headline that will determine if the email gets opened or not. Many people get dozens or even hundreds of emails each day, and if your email subject line is not compelling, it won't even get opened and all of the work you put into the design and copy of the email and landing page will be wasted. Consider testing your emails by sending them to a small subset of your list using different subject lines to optimize open response rates.

After the email is designed and written, it must be turned into HTML in order to get ready to be sent. During this production phase, make sure you thoroughly test the email to see how it renders in various emails and browsers, since there is no way to know the environment in which the user will read the email.

Today, most emails are read on mobile devices, so it's also very important to test the email on various mobile platforms such as iPhone, iPad, and Android devices to ensure that the email is readable and easy to use. It's also important to think about how you want users to respond from their mobile devices.

Filling out a long form to get a white paper or download a free software offer is much more difficult on an iPhone than a PC or Mac. Consider reducing the amount of form fields to be filled out and making call-to-action buttons larger when you are designing for mobile devices.

Personalization and Customization by Segment

People naturally respond better to emails that are created personally for them. If I receive an email that is addressed, "Dear David," I'm much more likely to pay attention than if it says, "Dear Sir." Worse still are emails that are addressed to "dreske," since it sounds like they just scrapped that from the first part of my email address.

If you have the names of your contacts in your list, definitely use them to personalize your emails. You can also use other information you have to personalize the email with their company name or the town they live in. Crafting a personalized email message will improve your results compared to generic messages.

Customization is when you send different emails to different users in your target audience. In order to do this, you first need to define your segments and then personalize your content accordingly in order to address their specific preferences.

In B2B markets, people commonly segment their audience based on industry and job function. This means that if you know that someone works in the financial services industry and is in sales, you'll use this information to customize the email for them in order to get a better response rate. You can do this by either creating separate emails for each segment, or by creating dynamic emails that are assembled as the emails are sent based on variables you set up in each email.

If you do this well, you'll create an email that is personalized and customized to the individual so that it's more relevant and you get a higher return on your email investment.

Social Sharing and Email

Social media is a very important tool to reach your audience and can be integrated into your email campaign in order to make each tool more effective. Sites such as Twitter, Facebook, YouTube, and LinkedIn are powerful ways to attract an audience and encourage the sharing of your content. here I'll share several ways that you can integrate your email and social media programs.

Social sharing tags are links that you can put in each of your emails that allow people to easily share your content with their followers on Twitter, Facebook, or LinkedIn. With one click, each of your readers can easily share your email with thousands of other people, so it's critical to make these links easy to see and encourage your readers to use them. Many email programs can track how many people share your email with their social media fans so that you can see the impact that these links have.

You can also send an email explicitly asking your email readers to follow you on your social media properties. This is like sending an email asking people to join another list, so include some kind of incentive if you can. This can take the form of a contest or small gift if they are willing to follow you. If you make this sound easy and fun, you'll be more successful in getting people to respond.

Integrating your Email Campaign with Search Marketing

Search marketing and web marketing are important tools that can help you build your email audience. The first step in integrating these two programs is to put a strong call to action on your website, similar to the types of offers you are using in your email campaigns. Then use search engine optimization (SEO) techniques to make your website more popular with the search engines to get more organic traffic.

You can also use paid search marketing (PPC) to drive traffic to your website and landing pages. This traffic will respond to your offers, convert on your landing pages, and build the audience for your email campaigns.

Email Execution—Software, Deliverability, Quality, Testing

Once your email is designed and written, it's time to send it. At this point it's tempting to feel that your job is done and you just need to hit the "send" button, but it's critical to work very carefully during this last phase of the email production process to ensure a high-quality campaign.

Once you send an email, there is no guarantee that it will be received by the user. Almost all organizations have spam filters that are designed to keep out unwanted email, but may also keep out your email.

All of the major Internet service providers (ISPs) also filter email. In the United States, the CAN SPAM law tried to define what spam is, but in practice, spam is whatever the Internet service providers stop from being sent to their users.

In order to ensure high email deliverability, you need to take several important steps. First, make sure your email is in compliance with the CAN SPAM law. This law has many provisions, but the most important provisions are that the subject line should not be deceptive, you must identify yourself with your company name and physical address in the email, and you need to give the user the option to opt-out of future emails.

Another key to high deliverability is to manage the quality of your list. If you have a very low open rate or response rate, the ISPs will consider your email to be spam. To keep this from happening, periodically purge from your list people who never respond. Why keep sending emails to people if they have not responded to any of your emails in the past year or two? This will also help boost your response rates in future email blasts.

A third key to ensuring high deliverability is to stay away from words and techniques which the spam filters looks for when deciding if email is spam or not. Some of these techniques include not using the word "free" in your email subject line, not using other phrases like "special offer" or "click here" or many words that are associated with sex or drugs. You should also avoid the use of all CAPS in your subject line. By staying away from this language, you'll be more likely to get your email delivered and read.

Email Is a Relationship

When you are building an email program it's important to remember that you are not shouting at your audience, you are building a relationship with them. As part of this relationship, you are giving them content and offers and asking them if they want to get more information or buy something that meets their needs.

This type of relationship works best when you give the recipient control over how often they hear from you, and what type of messages they will receive. One way to build this relationship is to use a "preference center" to let the user opt-out of some types of emails or get more or less frequent emails from you. If you don't let the user control the relationship, you risk losing them altogether when they get fed up and opt out.

Email Testing and Optimization

In every campaign, it's critical to test your emails in order to improve your results. Fortunately, there are many ways to test and optimize your email program.

The first step is to test your subject line. Each email you send should be randomly split into at least two subsets of your full list so that you can A/B test them against each other. Since the subject line determines if your recipient will open and read the email, use the open rate to evaluate the effectiveness of your subject line.

Just because one subject line gets a higher open rate than another doesn't necessarily mean that it's a winner. It's important to test the result to see if it's statistically significant. Even if you don't have a master's degree in statistics, you can use online tools to make sure you are getting good results in order to make a decision.

The variables you'll need to include are the number of impressions and the clicks or click-through rate of each of the tests. Once you have this, you'll be able to use an online calculator to get the degree of confidence that the winner is actually the winner.

You should look for 90–95% confidence using a statistical analysis tool before you can declare a winner.[15] If there is a winner, use it and

---

15   Source: HubSpot. Footnote at www.marketing-in-the-zone.com/footnotes

create a new test to see if you can improve the results. If there is no clear winner, you may need to retest with a larger sample size or a different creative in order to get a winner.

Tracking Email Campaign Performance

Once you have your campaign running, you'll want to track and report on the results in order to make informed decisions about how effective the campaign is. Key Performance Indicators (KPIs) are data about the campaign that you collect over time to decide if your campaign is on track. Some of the data you should track for in each campaign are:

- Email Sent—Your list should be growing over time with new people opting in.
- Open Rate—If your subject line is effective and relevant, your open rate will stay strong.
- Opt-out Rate—A high-quality list with strong emails will have a low opt-out rate.
- Click-through Rate—Well-designed emails with strong offers will have a high click-through rate because people will want to get more information.
- Conversion Rate—The conversion rate will tell you if your landing page and offers are strong.

It's critical to collect this data over time and make decisions regularly to improve and optimize the results. You won't always be right, but at least you'll have very clear feedback on your decisions.

Email Marketing Summary

High-performance email marketing campaigns can be optimized to build your audience, improve deliverability, and get good engagement through email opens and conversions in order to drive good business results. By using the techniques described in this chapter, you can develop a strong and effective email marketing program.

When you build consistent, strong results every time, you'll get in the Zone. By understanding your audience and delivering what they need with well-crafted emails, you can be confident and happy that your program is a success.

Email Marketing Automation
in the Zone

T he leads you collect today aren't necessarily ready to buy immediately. Some of them are, of course, but others may still be researching products or solutions and are not ready to make a purchase decision. Your existing customers may also be leads for other products you sell, or be interested in buying more of the products or services they already buy. Email Marketing Automation programs are excellent ways to nurture buyers through the buying process quickly and cost-effectively.

Joel's Email Marketing Automation Program

As a senior executive at a large insurance company that sells through a community of independent insurance agents, Joel needed to increase revenue. He needed to stay in front of his agents with the latest insurance offers, so he was sending 3–4 emails per week to the agents with very repetitive sales messages. As a result, his emails were getting only a .2% click-through rate. That means that he only got 2 clicks for every thousand emails he was sending. By any measure, this was a pretty anemic campaign.

In order to get better engagement, we worked with Joel to change the email strategy from pure promotional messages to a series of informative articles that educated the agents about important trends in the insurance industry. The articles features stories of difficult-to-place insurance, which taught the agents how to work with some of the premiere companies in their industry. By changing the email content and strategy, the click-through rate increased dramatically.

Joel didn't want to just educate the agents, however, he wanted to get them engaged. To do this, we set up the program to automatically send a series of four email messages that sold them on the unique benefits of his agency after an agent clicked on the first email.

The new follow-up campaign got a click-through rate of 15%, or 75 times the original click-through rate. Clearly the new email strategy was educating the agents and getting them engaged so that quote requests increased dramatically. Joel moved from frustration and confusion to a place in the Zone where he was confident that his email program was driving engagement and leads.

Marketing Automation Strategy

A solid marketing automation program can shorten your sales cycle and let you generate additional revenue. The lead you collect today is a lead that may need to be gently and strategically nurtured to become a customer.

In order to build a strong program to nurture leads, you need to take the following steps:

You will probably start implementing a lead nurture program using email, so it's important to use all of the email best practices I discussed in the previous chapter. Keep in mind, however, that you can also nurture leads through search marketing and social media using many of the same techniques.

Market Segments

Before you sign the license agreement and create the PO for a new marketing automation tool to manage your lead nurture program, you'll need to think about the goals of the program and the audience for the campaign. Are you going to focus on prospects who've signed up on your website, prospects generated by your sales team, an existing list of prospects, current customers, or new customers? Each of these audiences has a different relationship with your company and very different needs.

You may also want to look at different segments within these groups. Will the campaign be more effective if you address them by industry, or by their job function or level within the organization?

Your sales team probably does this very naturally, so you may want to interview them to see how it's done. Before your best sales people deliver their pitch, it's natural for them to ask a series of questions so that they can respond with a message that is specifically tailored to the prospect.

Marketing automation software for lead nurture can mimic this process and you can set it up so that it happens quickly and easily without human intervention. This way, your sales team can spend their time closing deals and working with their best customers, and not doing the mundane work of sending emails to each new lead.

The Buying Cycle

As I described in the chapter on marketing strategy, each product or service you sell has a specific buying cycle and companies describe them in variety of ways. A common way to think about it is using the following sequence:

- Awareness—In this phase, the prospects are trying to understand what they need, and what potential solutions exist.
- Consideration—In this phase, they are evaluating alternative solutions to their problem.
- Purchase—In this phase, prospects are evaluating products from different companies to decide which one to buy.

We all go through this decision process for our own consumer purchases, and organizations go through the same steps for larger business purchases.

Let's say that I'm interested in buying a new video camera for personal use. I have a camera now that is five years old and somehow feel that there should be something better on the market. My first step in the awareness phase would be to do some research to see what's new in video camera technology and features.

I'll be asking questions like:

- What is the best screen resolution available?
- What types of zoom lenses are there?
- Who are the major manufacturers?
- How do cameras connect to social media sites and my wireless network?

Once I get answers to these questions, I'll finish the awareness phase with a good understanding of what's available and what I need.

After I do some research to understand these issues, I'll move into the consideration phase. In this phase, I'll look at different alternatives from the manufacturers I researched in the first phase, and get more detailed information.

I may watch a video showcasing how their current customers use the product and I'll probably try one out for myself at a store. Ideally, I'll come out of the consideration phase with a good understanding of the one or two products that I want to buy.

In the last phase, purchase, I want to buy the product I'm interested in at the best price. I might go to a store or two and shop online to find the best price from a supplier I trust with the service, warranty, and payment options that are best for me.

Once you understand the buying process, you can use this knowledge to design a series of emails to move the buyer through the process with the right content at the right time, so that they buy from you. If you don't do this well, you may turn off your prospect and they may opt-out of your communication stream. For example, if I register to receive more information at the time I'm researching technology and features, and the manufacturer sends me a "coupon" deal, it might accelerate my purchase, but more than likely, I won't be ready.

Ideally you should send a series of email messages and content that gradually moves your prospects through the buying cycle over time. In the example above, a series of content that might be appropriate would be: a technology guide on HD video or lens quality, followed by a comparison guide or user testimonial, and finally a discount or a free shipping offer to encourage a purchase.

The manufacturer can't know exactly how fast I will move through the buying cycle, but at least they will be sending me a stream of relevant content that's appropriate to the way most people buy. They can also ask me where I am in the buying process as they send me more content.

Although this sounds simple enough, most companies simply send the same content to their entire list over and over again. Clearly, a personalized strategy based on the buying cycle stands a better chance of success.

Emails and Offers

The next step is to create emails and offers specific to the buying cycle for each segment you want to address with your campaign. For each phase of the buying cycle, you'll need to create an offer, a landing page, and email that address the unique needs of the buyer.

As you can see, this can start to turn into a lot of emails. If you plan to send six emails to three segments, you'll need to create 18 emails for the campaign. If you add another variable, such as customization by industry, or by size of company or job function, you will need to create many more. Fortunately, after you produce the emails, you can load them into your marketing automation platform, which makes it much easier to send individual emails to all of these types of people.

Touch Points, Timing, and Triggers

When you are setting up a nurture campaign, you need to decide how many touch points you will create for the program. Will you send three follow-up emails, or six, or 20? The number of emails you decide on will depend on the complexity of the sale and the length of the buying cycle. The longer the cycle, the more you'll want to send over time.

Timing is also important. Will you send emails every day, every two days, or once a week? Again, that depends on how many messages you will be sending and over what time period. For most campaigns, weekly touch points work fine. You should avoid sending emails to your list too frequently, as this increases the risk of high opt-out rates. You'll also need to consider how long the campaign will last. Will you send messages over two weeks, two months, or a year?

Triggers are additional emails that can be sent based on specific activity taken by the user. This activity can be a website visit, or even clicking on a specific page. For example, if I'm receiving early stage technology emails about my camcorder purchase and then one day I visit the pricing section of the website, the company can set up the system to automatically send me a "free shipping" message since I may be farther down the cycle than it thought.

Triggers can be powerful tools, but you should avoid making it feel too much like "Big Brother" is watching. In the example above, you would not want to say, "I noticed that you visited the pricing page and you may be interested in…" You can be more general and still make people feel that you are speaking to them personally.

One campaign we recently created for a client used four touch points sent over a two-month period of time with an additional trigger message that was sent the day after the user revisited the website.

Email Creative

Once you have your lead nurture strategy in place, the next step in the process is to actually design the email templates and write all of the content. This may include offers like white papers or user guides, or it could be more media-intensive with video, infographics, or other interactive tools. Remember that the stronger the offer, the better the response rate. In addition to creating the email, you may also need to create the landing pages and thank you pages for the campaign.

Marketing Automation Software

Once you have the emails and landing pages written and produced, it's time to load them into a marketing automation tool. These software platforms will connect to both your website and CRM system, and make it easy for you to set up the email campaigns, triggers, and move leads into the CRM system when they are ready.

Part of the setup will include linking the offers and landing pages on your website to the automation tool so that your lead nurture program will start when a new user registers. You can also load existing contacts in the system to move your house email list down the lead nurturing path.

The software will also give you the ability to set up the marketing automation rules I've discussed above. For example, you can tell the system to send the first nurture email two days after a user registers and the next touch point seven days later. You can also put in logic that prevents an email from being sent if the user visits a specific web page or is contacted by the sales team.

Many of these systems also include a lead scoring capability, which watches the user's behavior as they respond to emails or visit the website and assigns the user a score based on criteria you define. You can then set triggers based on that score, such as asking a sales person to call.

Manage and Optimize the Lead Nurture Program

Once you have the strategy in place, the content created, and the system designed, it's time to start using it. You can kick off the campaign with your in-house email list and start watching as emails get sent to people who register on your website.

The software will give you all of the reporting you'd expect from an email system, such as open rates, click-through rates, opt-out and conversion rates. Based on this data, you can continuously work to improve the program by removing emails and offers that are not performing well, and testing new content. You can also see if entire segments are not performing as well as others, and redesign the strategy for that group if necessary.

Accelerating your Lead Nurture Program

A fully implemented lead nurture program gives you the ability to quickly and easily follow-up with leads in a way that naturally moves them through the buying cycle. If designed properly, it will increase the number of quality leads and sales, and enable you to be as thorough as possible in communicating with your potential customers, all with much less time and effort than is required from traditional marketing techniques.

You will know you are on your way when you've covered the entire buying process and all of your target markets with strong messages and good offers. And you'll be rewarded with good click-through rates, engagement, leads, and sales. This should give you strong results and a feeling of confidence, which means you are in the Zone.

Social Media Marketing
in the Zone

Social Media Marketing Strategy

Social media marketing has become one of the most important marketing techniques. Facebook now has over 1.7 billion users, Instagram has 400 million, Twitter has 320 million, and LinkedIn has 100 million members.[16] There are over 2.2 billion active social media users worldwide[17].

Social media traffic has accounted for almost all Internet traffic growth in the past five years. As newspaper readers and TV viewers decline, social media usage continues to grow rapidly. Today, 65% of the United States' online adults use social media—a nearly 10-fold jump in the last 10 years. [18] With so many users on social media sites, there's no question that your target audience is using social media.

16   Source: Statista. Footnote at www.marketing-in-the-zone.com/footnotes
17   Source: Social Media Today. Footnote at www.marketing-in-the-zone.com/footnotes .
18   Source: Pew Research Center. Footnote at www.marketing-in-the-zone.com/footnotes

Social media can be a very powerful tool for every organization, from the very large to the very small. It lets you drive more traffic to your website, and engage with your customers and prospects in a more personal and powerful way. Because of all of this, social media marketing should be part of every high-performance marketer's toolkit.

Amy's Social Media Marketing Program

Amy was the Director of Corporate Communications at a division of a large telecommunications company. Her division used many traditional marketing vehicles including PR, analyst relations, events, and brand advertising to reach their target audience and drive leads. While she was very professional in all of her work, she was uneasy with the fact that few of these programs produced any measurable results. She wanted to get more engagement through social media platforms, but the social media team at her HQ kept a tight rein on their social media programs, so very little of her content made it into their channels.

We got involved with Amy and built new social media channels for her division including Facebook, Twitter, and LinkedIn properties. By having independent channels, she was able to reach out to specific customers and influencers in the media and analyst community to build engagement and influence.

Once the properties were ready, we started the process of building her follower base by reaching out to everyone in her community who was talking about the issues she cared about. As we followed these people, many followed back and we grew her follower base from 1,000 to over 11,000 in two years. We also posted over 200 times per month with a mix of industry content, branded content, and promotional content to make her social media sites the source of relevant and high-quality information for her target audience.

Amy's social media campaigns drive thousands of visits to the website from prospects and customers, and Amy went from feeling inadequate and behind the times, to feeling very confident the she had built a communications platform for her company that would deliver value for years to come.

Social Media Marketing Goals

A high-performance social media marketing program is focused on leveraging the power and reach of social media platforms to achieve your business goals. The best social media goals are measurable and are tied to actual metrics such as "achieve 100 mentions of my brand on Twitter and blogs by the third month of the program," or "increase traffic to my site from social media sites to 1,000 visits per month and convert this to 50 leads." Or better yet, "get 50 leads that convert into 15 new clients in the next three months." Once you have a good understanding of your goals, you'll be better able to organize your activity around them to achieve business results.

When you focus on your goals, you'll learn which posts drive the most leads and sales. You'll also be able to grow the number of fans and followers with people who are most likely to buy your products. This approach is different from an activity-based social media campaign that measures success by the number of social media posts. It gives you the data you need to make good decisions that will bring in more customers over time.

Social Media Strategy

In order to create an effective social media strategy, you need to have clear goals, listen to what your customers and prospects are saying, understand your customers, and assess your own team and content.

Once you have the strategy right, you can develop your platforms, create content, grow your followers, and engage your audience.

Understand your Audience

Once you understand your goals, it's critical to understand your audience. Will you be speaking to a B2B audience or B2C? Which industry, demographic, and locations do they represent?

Since social media communication can be personal and informal, it's helpful to create several profiles or personas that represent the different segments you'll be communicating with. By using the Persona development process I discussed earlier, you'll be able to create a more nuanced view of your target audience and create better content for them.

For example, if you are selling to the IT market, you might invent "Susan," the 45-year-old CIO of a medium-sized company, and "Terry," the Database Consultant. When you start to think about the content that your market needs, it's easier if you can personalize it by thinking of what Susan and Terry might need.

Active Listening

An important step in preparing to launch your campaign is listening to your market. What are they saying about your company, your competitors, and the issues you care about? To get a pulse of the market, subscribe to groups on LinkedIn or Facebook, and set up Twitter lists to get a constant stream of what the market is talking about.

Competitive Analysis and Benchmarking

Since most of the Internet is public, you can get a good understanding of what your competitors are doing with social media and learn from them before you launch. To get started, look at their Twitter, Facebook, Instagram, LinkedIn, and YouTube Accounts. Look at what they are saying, how many fans and followers they have, and who is following them.

Identify Available Content

Social media programs require a lot of content, so instead of planning to create everything from scratch, take an inventory of what already exists that you can use for this program. Do you have video, white papers, presentations, case studies, web pages, articles, or even press releases that can be repurposed for your social media campaign?

You may not want to take a two-year-old case study and pass it off as new content, but there is no reason you can't repackage key facts in the case study for a series of Tweets, or even promote it again on Twitter. You should build as comprehensive an inventory of content as possible so that you can avoid recreating the wheel and hit the ground running with a stream of strong content.

Identify Internal Leaders & Spokespeople

Social media is very personal. Your readers will want to know who they are talking to, and learn as much about them as possible. It's important, therefore, to recruit a group of internal leaders who can act as spokespeople for the campaign. It's wonderful if your CEO is a gifted writer and can invest time for the social media campaign, but it's also fine to have a group of other executives who will participate in the program over time.

Identify Influencers and Leading Sites

To get leverage in a social media program, you'll want to get other industry influencers to talk about you and share your content with their audience. You can find these people by searching for Twitter or LinkedIn users in your industry.

You can also search for people in your industry in a service called Klout, which ranks their overall influence. Since you have limited time to build relationships with influencers, spend your time getting the most influential people in your industry with the highest Klout scores to like and promote your content.

Develop Policies and Workflow

The final step of preparation for a successful social media campaign is to develop the internal policies and workflow you'll need to manage the program. For some companies, this is a simple as using the popular motto, "do no harm," and setting them free to connect as they think best.

Other organizations, especially large ones, will need to create a social media policy document which defines what can and cannot be shared on social media. If you have multiple people involved in the program, or if you are working with an outside vendor, you'll also need to create an approval workflow to make sure that the right people approve content that is posted on social media pages.

In a simple example, your Director of Marketing may be empowered to create and post content as she feels is appropriate, assuming full accountability for results. In a complex example, you may have a copywriter or outside agency create content, send it to the Director of Marketing for content approval, then to your in-house counsel for legal approval before it's sent back to the agency to be posted. Obviously, the second approach won't be as spontaneous and responsive as the first, but if legal approval is important in your industry, then you'll need to live with it.

Whatever your policies or processes, it's important to document them so that employees are protected and everyone is on the same page.

Creating Social Media Platforms

Now that you've build your strategy, you are ready for the next step of creating the actual social media properties. Many people think this is the fun part since it's when your ideas turn into designs, graphics, content, and web pages on the social media sites.

The first step is to decide which sites you are going to use. The most popular sites are Facebook, YouTube, Twitter, and LinkedIn. Instagram, Snapchat and Pinterest are gaining major popularity among brands. Even though these are the top sites, you don't need to use all of these, and you can add others if you feel that there is a site that's more appropriate in your industry. B2C firms often skip using LinkedIn and B2B firms often skip using Instagram. I believe that both of these sites can be used for any industry, but if you have limited resources, this is a good guideline.

With each of these sites, you'll need to register and secure a page with the name of your company. If your preferred name is already taken, then choose something close that is short, makes sense, and is easy for your readers to remember.

Most of the channels allow you to create custom designs and graphics to improve your branding on otherwise bland pages. You should definitely take advantage of this option by creating a strong design that engages the user.

Each of the social media sites needs to be thought of as a unique "micro site" with special design and content needs.

Twitter and YouTube both offer the opportunity to create a custom design background to reinforce your brand and give the user additional information about you. Facebook lets you create banners and graphics that tell your story.

LinkedIn lets you create custom product pages that give more detail on your company, products, and services. In all of these sites, make sure you provide the user with all of the information you can. Writing the content for these sites is a little like writing a small website, so plan time to create the content you need.

Create Your Editorial Content Calendar

Once you have the sites set up, it's time to develop a plan to create and distribute the content. For some companies, that means creating all new content, while others have a great deal of content that can be repurposed for the social media campaign.

Some organizations take a casual approach to creating content, while others are much more deliberate. In the casual approach, you may look at your accounts every day and decide what content to write and post. This approach allows you to be very dynamic and responsive to content you see across the Internet. Your content will be very fresh, but it can also be stressful to think of new ideas for content and posts each day.

A more deliberate approach would be to create an editorial calendar that will become your guide to the themes for each day or each week. You can organize your editorial calendar around content like white papers and webinars, or around events such as conferences and trade shows. By knowing what your core content or themes are each week, you'll be able to be more thorough in covering your subjects. It's also easier to include others in the content creation process, since you can schedule specific contributors into your schedule.

It's helpful to manage the editorial calendar in monthly and quarterly views. By planning one to three months ahead, you can take into account new product launches, events, and other activities that will drive new content for you.

Just because you have an editorial calendar doesn't mean that you won't be dynamic or responsive to the market. It just gives you a framework to guide all of your content creation activities.

When you build your content plan, remember that you won't need to develop all of your own content. It's perfectly acceptable to repurpose other people's content within your campaign. This serves two purposes. First, by posting links to other good content, you'll position your company as a thought leader and expert in the industry. Second, the organization whose content you promote will recognize the traffic you are sending to them and be more likely to repost your content. This is a very important way to get broader distribution for your content.

Before you launch your social media properties, make sure you set up tracking so that you can see the impact of your work. Two tools that are very helpful here are URL shortening tools and website analytics tools.

URL shorteners allow you to track the number of people that click on the links in your Tweets and posts. They also shorten the URLs you use to make them fit in sites like Twitter that impose character constraints on the content you post.

Website analytics programs like Google Analytics enable you to see the impact of your work on website traffic and your goals. Once you set it up properly, you'll be able to see how much traffic comes back to your website from each social media site, what those visitors did once they got to your site, and how many goal conversions resulted from your social media activities.

Another key step before you launch is to make sure that your website and landing pages are integrated with your social media program. It's easy to put social media sharing tags on your landing pages, emails, and home page to allow people to share your content with their network. You should also give people the ability to follow you from your website and emails.

Grow your Followers

While you are posting content and interacting with your audience, it's critical to build a base of fans and followers or you may find that your social media work will have very little impact on your business. Unless you have thousands of fans, it's unlikely that your posts will generate much of an impact.

Let's use a simple example to illustrate the math here. If you are posting two Tweets every business day (40 Tweets per month) and have 500 Twitter followers, then you have the potential to make 20,000 impressions per month. (In practice, you may get more because of retweets and search, but we'll leave that out of this example.) If you can increase your follower base to 10,000 followers, then you have the potential to get 400,000 impressions with no additional effort.

If your click-through rate on Tweets is .1%, in the first example you'll generate 20 clicks to your website per month and in the second example, you'll generate 400. In order to make an impact on your business, you'll need to get a large number of fans and followers.

Here are four ways to build you follower and fan base:

1. **Follow the right people.** When you follow people on Twitter, they often follow you back, so the key is to follow the right people. Start by searching for people with the right titles who are working for the companies you are interested in, and follow them. You can also follow people that post content at one of your industry trade shows or events. Another strategy is to follow people that follow your competitors or industry luminaries.

   After you follow these people, monitor whether they follow you back. If they don't, stop following them and start following others. You can repeat this process over and over as you build up your base.

2. **Create content that is worth sharing.** Great content can build your follower base exponentially, and we call this "going viral." If you create a video, coupon, article, white paper, or other content that people get excited about, they will share them with

their own friends and followers. This means that even if you only have a few thousand followers, your offer can be seen by millions of people within a few days.

It's often hard to predict the content that will go viral, but you should try to be a creative as possible to develop content that will reach this threshold, because it can dramatically accelerate your social media growth if you do.

3. **Other Promotions.** There are many ways to promote your social media presence in order to build your follower base. Before you use these other promotional techniques, be sure to think about what's in it for the user, not just what's in it for your company. Will they get access to great content, coupons, or inside information? If you have something special that you can offer them, then you'll have a better chance of creating a meaningful and powerful call to action.

One obvious place to promote your social media presence is on your website. It's easy to put the icons for your social media sites in a prominent place on your website, but you should also consider ways to promote the social media icons to help improve the click-through rate and your overall followers.

Email can be another important way to promote your social media presence. You should put the social media icons and links on every email to encourage content sharing and more followers.

Another great place to promote your properties is by integrating them into your direct customer contact. By training your sales and customer service teams to point people to your social media sites, you'll build up a base of very high-quality followers.

4. **Advertise.** If the previous three ideas don't produce enough followers fast enough, then advertising can help. You can

advertise on social media sites and link the ads back to your social media properties. The chapter on Social Advertising has more detail on this subject.

Engage your Audience

Now that you've created your presence on social media sites, you are ready to start syndicating your content and building your followers.

When you post content to the various social media sites you've created, it's a good idea to customize it whenever you can. If you are posting to Twitter, you need to limit your post to 140 characters, but you'll have more room on LinkedIn or Facebook, so use it if you have something important to say.

You can also take advantage of tools that allow you to post content once, and then have it automatically flow to other sites. For example, you may want to set up your Twitter account to automatically take your LinkedIn posts and display them there. This will save you time and make it easier to leverage the work you are doing to build content on various sites at the same time.

Most of your content will be appropriate for you own properties, but don't forget to post content to groups or blogs where it's appropriate. This can often give you much broader reach than posting only to your own properties, especially at first when you don't have many followers and fans.

As you get more engaged with groups, you may want to alter your content calendar to develop more content that's appropriate for groups, since it often needs to be less self-promotional. These groups can be wonderful places to build your reputation with your target audience and encourage them to follow you.

Interaction on social media sites is much more than a one-way conversation. In many ways, you should think of this as two-way conversation in a live group setting. If you walk into a networking event and only talk about yourself, you'll be soon considered boring and self-centered. The result will be that you'll have few friends and you'll spend most of your time talking to yourself.

In a social situation, you'll do much better if you listen as much as you talk, and if you're as interested in commenting on others' success as you are interested in your own.

These same principles apply to social media. The more interactive and interested you can be with others; the more engaged people will be with you.

All users, of course, are not equally influential, so pay special attention to people with large groups of fans and followers. It will make a much bigger impact if you can engage a person with 25,000 followers as opposed to a person with just 500 followers. Focus on the most important people, but engage with everyone you can, and you'll be seen as a friendly, easy person to connect with.

As you interact with people, it's also important to notice and respond to what others are saying with personal comments. These types of posts can make you seem real and approachable. It may feel like you are using social media site as you would email to say "thanks" or "nice work," but remember that others will see this and it will enhance your reputation.

Optimize the Campaign

Once you have the campaign up and running and you're gaining fans and followers, it's time to start optimizing the campaign in both quantity and quality. By this I mean that you should look at the most important metrics and use what you learn to improve the results of the campaign.

To improve the campaign quantitatively, you'll need to collect important metrics, including the number of content posts, followers and likes, website visits, and conversions. By tracking these metrics, you'll be able to see how effective you are at driving fans and followers, and how people respond to your content.

Social media, of course, it not just about the numbers. You also need to see which content is most effective at driving results. You can track the click-through rate for various types of posts and then see which drives the best results.

For example, do press releases, product announcements, free content, or coupon offers drive the best results? Or is there a specific topic or message that people respond to? By tracking the response rate for these various types of content, you'll be able to see which work best and adjust your editorial calendar accordingly.

Another important part of managing an ongoing social media program is responding to comments and feedback. The more interaction you have with your audience, the more effective the campaign. The interaction may take the form of comments on your blog or Facebook page, or direct messages on Twitter.

Whatever the interaction, it's important to personally address each one to make people feel like you are listening and interested in what they have to say, since those people may be important influencers who could help spread your word to thousands.

Maximize Your Impact

In any social media campaign, you will create an impact through both high-quality and a large quantity of content. Every program starts with listening to the conversations about your brand and the issues you care about. Once you understand how and where to engage, you'll be able to create and syndicate content to a variety of social media properties in order to drive traffic to your website.

As you work this engine, you'll see that your social media marketing program can produce a measurable ROI. To start, you need to take your general business goals and translate them into specific, measurable goals that can be tracked and reported on. You also need to organize your activities and content to drive the traffic and the results you want.

Integrating Search with Social Media

Search marketing is critical to the success of any social media marketing program because you must be found in order for your content to have an impact. Social media can be a powerful accelerator to any paid or organic search marketing program.

Here are eight ways to integrate your social media program into your search marketing campaign:

1. **Leverage video on search landing pages.** If you are creating video for your YouTube program, you can also create short videos to promote the offers on your landing pages. Those offers might be white papers, free trials, offers for a consultation, or even a coupon, and they can all be promoted using a video. Video makes it more personal and engaging and will improve the conversion rate on the landing page.

2. **Leverage offer comments and ratings on search landing pages.** Just as people rate travel sites and other online content, you can let people rate the content and offers on your website. This builds trust and engagement. When people see the rankings on your content, they will have a much stronger sense of where to spend their time. Naturally, some of your content will rank high and others not so high, but this honesty will build trust with your readers.

3. **Advertise on Facebook and other social media sites.** Most of this chapter has been about using content to connect with your audience on social media sites, but you can also complement this free content with paid advertising. Facebook, LinkedIn, YouTube, and most others accept advertising and allow very specific targeting since they have detailed information on their users. You can use these ads for a variety of purposes, including

bringing users back to your website, increasing engagement, and building your follower base.

4. **Leverage social media sharing on landing pages.** Most landing pages are designed to "convert" the user from a visitor to a customer or lead, so they are short and promote a specific piece of content. If the content is valuable, people will want to share it, so make it easy for them by including sharing tags on your landing page or thank you page.

5. **Embed your SEO keywords into video posts and other content posts.** It's important for your social media content to get found, so use the keywords you've identified on all of your video posts or on specific social media content. When you include these keywords, add them to links if possible to make them more prominent to the search engines.

6. **Write keyword-filled content for social media sites with links.** Keywords are also important when you are writing content for your own sites, or posting as comments on other blogs. By including the keywords with links back to your site, you'll be telling the search engines that you are an authority for these keywords. When you do this well, you'll get more traffic from both the links you embed in other social media sites and also from the increased keyword visibility that comes indirectly from getting better link popularity.

7. **Build links from social media—optimized press releases.** Another great source of links are press releases. When you distribute a press release through a tool such as Business Wire or PR Newswire, you can include social media content such as videos and photos with links that will improve your search engine visibility.

8. **Build links from articles, blog comments, and content distribution.** Along with press releases, you can also embed

links in articles and blog comments that you can distribute for free. These articles can be repurposed from your blog or as part of a white paper or webinar. When you distribute them to article sites, include links with keywords embedded that make you look more powerful with the search engines.

How to Social Media Optimize your Website

Your website can also be an important way for people to get involved with your social media program. The first step is to let your website visitors share and bookmark your content with "add-this" www.addthis.com or "share this" www.sharethis.com. There should be persistent links out to social networks from every page of your website. When you do this, it's important to make sure that your brand and social media presence is consistent on both sites.

Another way to build social media into your website is to build transparency and the human element with videos, photo sharing, profiles of your team, customer's profiles, video case studies, and/or product reviews.

A prominent feature of all social media properties is that you feel like you know the person you are interacting with better when you see their picture and know something about their personal and professional interests.

Most websites, however, are very sterile, and tell you very little about the people behind the company or the website. By including more content about the management team (or others), it will make the website seem more authentic and approachable.

Social media programs are very dynamic, with new content being added every day. Websites, however, are often static. One way to leverage social media content on your website is to add unique RSS feeds from social networks like Twitter, Facebook, LinkedIn, and blogs in categories that align to your website's content, and open your thought-leadership content like white papers and articles up for discussion on those networks. This will bring fresh content to your website automatically and give your users yet another reason to visit your pages.

Social Media is More Than Just Marketing

I've discussed a number of ways that social media can be effective as a marketing tool, but keep in mind that there are also very important ways to use it for customer service, product development, sales, purchasing, and recruiting. By thinking of social media holistically, you'll realize that it can permeate every aspect of your company's work.

Your customer service team is focused on responding to customer issues and resolving them quickly and cost-effectively. Today, customers may not only complain directly, they may also complain publicly on Twitter or other sites, so that their frustrations can reach thousands of other people who follow them.

It's important for your customer service team to monitor your company's brand on social media sites and then interact directly with these people to resolve the issues. One benefit of this approach is that their followers will see how you respond and may feel better about your product or brand. People often expect problems with products or services, but they can be completely blown away by excellent service to fix a problem.

Product development teams can monitor the same stream of content for insight into product usage issues or frustrations that may lead to new features, products, or services. They can also monitor what your competitors or their customers are talking about, and gain insight into their future plans. Social media can also be a great resource for getting feedback from the marketplace on potential new product features or service changes.

The sales team can effectively use social media in many ways. When prospecting, they can use tools like LinkedIn to identify potential customers, connect with them through their network, and then reach out to them. They can also learn more about their professional background and personal interests, which may make it easier for them to build a relationship and turn the prospect into a customer. By listening to their social media comments and posts, they will be able to get a better understanding of their needs and wants, which should also help build a relationship.

A note of caution here: if people feel that you are stalking them or they are being "spammed" because you've found them on social media, you can create a very negative backlash. People don't want to feel that their privacy is being violated or that they are being manipulated, so be careful with how you use personal information.

Your purchasing team can use social media to find reviews and feedback before making important selections for products and services. Once they find relevant comments, they can also find other users and get personal feedback.

In the past, vendors would provide a list of references that were vetted and happy. Now your purchasing team can go beyond this sanitized list to find other customers and get the real story. This puts a lot of pressure on the customer service team of any company to manage their digital reputation to make sure that there are no lingering, unanswered negative comments, reviews, or ratings.

Social media sites can also be used by your recruiting team when they are looking for candidates. Just as the sales team can find potential customers on LinkedIn through targeted searching, the recruiting team can do the same. They can identify potential candidates and then approach them by phone or email to see if they are interested in exploring opportunities with your company.

Once you find people, you can learn more about them through their social media postings. Recruiters will want to see if the candidates have the kind of reputation that will make them a good employee or if there are any red flags that might need to be discussed during an interview. Candidates should make sure that they understand their privacy settings on sites like Facebook, so that they only share images and information that they want to share with the public—including potential employers.

Social Media Marketing Strategy

Because of its broad reach and immediate impact, social media marketing should be part of every marketer's strategy. You can use it to broadly engage with your market, build your brand, drive leads, increase sales, and grow your business. If you take the steps I've outlined here, I'm sure you'll soon be building a solid program and you'll feel like you are in the Zone.

Testing and Optimization in the Zone

Digital marketing makes it possible to easily create tests to learn what works best in order to improve the results of your marketing programs. The nature of digital marketing means you can test almost anything about your campaign. Testing offers, key messages, ad copy, graphic design, headlines, and every other element is not only possible, but easier and much less expensive than with traditional media.

Just because you can test anything, however, does not mean you should, and what you test and how you test will determine how effective you are at improving your results. After all, no one has an unlimited testing budget, and even if you did, it's important to test the variables that can have the largest impact first in order to use that information to get better results faster.

Here are the steps to creating an effective testing program.

| Test Strategy | Test Ideas and Hypothesis | Develop Test Assets | Implement Test Platform | Analyze Results |

Jacob's Testing Experience

Jacob was the CMO of a large list management company that owned the contact information for millions of people and rented marketing and sales lists to organizations of every size. He had very large competitors with big marketing budgets, and we needed to make the most of his marketing funds.

We were already managing his digital ad campaigns, but Jacob was unsure if the program was as effective as possible. He wanted to get more leads for each dollar spent.

As we developed the campaigns, we made many decisions along the way about the best keywords, messages, ad copy, offers and landing pages to use. Now that all of this was set up, Jacob wanted to begin systematically testing every variable.

We started by developing a test strategy and test hypothesis, listing all of the variations to test, and creating a test plan. Once we completed each test we documented the results and provided recommendations for further testing. It was very interesting to see that many variables like the color of the landing pages, or the images we chose made very little difference. The biggest impact came when we tested sending traffic directly to a landing page instead of sending it to the company's home page. We found that we improved results by 800% by using dedicated landing pages.

The testing program improved Jacob's marketing results, but he also learned a lot and it gave him the confidence that we were running a very efficient and effective campaign.

Jacob moved from a feeling of anxiety to a sense of mastery of the marketing program that brought him into the Zone.

Test Strategy

Before you begin creating your first test asset or installing testing software, you need to identify clear goals for your tests. Do you want to improve click-through rates, lead conversion rates, or increase actual sales revenue? Are you trying to learn which messaging is most effective or drive more leads? Once you identify your goals, you'll be able to create a test plan that achieves your goals. As you do this, you should also do the math to see the impact that you might make with your test plan. In other words, how much more money would you make if you improve your conversion rate by 25%, and is this worth the cost of the test?

Test Ideas Hypothesis

When testing, you must start with a test hypothesis, which is a question you want to answer. If you can't frame your test into a meaningful question, then you can't really develop the test properly. The test hypothesis might include tests of the design, structure, copy, or offers on your website or the ads you are running. The goal of this exercise is to identify the most likely changes that are going to have the greatest impact so you can test them first.

What Not to Test

The first thing you need to understand when building a test plan is what not to test. Don't test things that are unlikely to make a difference. Should your banner be red or blue? Should the submit button be round or rectangular? These changes are unlikely to produce significant results, so test them after you test the biggest, most important questions you have.

Another place to avoid testing is an area we call "best practices." If other people have already tested something and published data that tells you it works, then use their experience and don't make these things the first thing you test. An example of this would be landing page design. A best-practice landing page should have a good offer with a strong call to action, the form above the fold at the top of the page, and a limited amount of copy.

Don't start by testing a bad offer, with no call to action, a form buried deep down the page and thousands of words of copy against the good page. You'll just be wasting your time.

By leveraging experts in design and direct marketing you can save yourself tens of thousands of dollars and many hours, and arrive at the answer much faster. So do your homework first and leverage all of the expert advice and best practice experience that you can.

After you've done all of this, you'll still find that there are many things you'll want to test.

Everyone Gets an Opinion—Then Test

A good place to start building a test plan is the disagreements you have with your team on what will make a strong campaign. One person will often feel strongly that one topic or offer is best. Another person might strongly believe that one media type is best. Still another person will feel that certain creative designs will perform best.

Many times these arguments can be diffused through testing. People often believe strongly that their ideas are best because they've had experience doing something that's worked or not worked, even though they have not really tested it scientifically. These ideas are often good, and it's fine to build them into your test plan.

Good Things to Test

In my experience, the best things to test are the things that are likely to make the most difference the fastest. In most programs, this includes the offer itself, the advertising media, the targeting variables, and the creative.

The Offer

The offer is almost always the most important element of the campaign. What are you asking the user to do? What is their incentive to do it? If you are running a B2B campaign and offering a white paper in exchange for the user's contact information, then it's critical to offer content that is valuable, timely, and important. An offer can be early-stage content such as a white paper, mid-stage content such as a case study or demo, or a late-stage offer such as a sales meeting.

The Media

The media you choose to use for your campaign is one of the most important decisions you will make. If you choose to advertise on billboards when newspaper ads, tradeshow ads, or Internet banner ads would have been more effective, you can waste a lot of money quickly.

The problem with media decisions is that they are often relatively expensive and any one item can take a large portion of your budget, so unless you have a very large budget, you can only choose a few items to test. It can also take a lot of effort to evaluate and then manage each media purchase, and then collect and analyze the data.

When choosing media, it's important to evaluate each option on similar criteria, and then make decisions based on your ultimate goal. This will make it easier to set up the tracking mechanisms you need to evaluate the results once the campaign is over.

If your goal is to drive qualified leads for your sales team, then create a simple table to evaluate all of your media choices. The table will include the name, cost, number of impressions, clicks or contacts expected, leads expected, and cost per lead expected. By collecting the data across your media options based on your goals, you'll be able to rank order the use of media based on which will produce the most leads or which will produce the lowest cost per lead.

Paid vs. Earned Media

Today, paid media are only a small portion of your media options. If you are active with your website or social media, you'll also need to manage your investments in time and energy in non-paid media such as social networking sites, your own website, micro sites, partner sites, and press activity. These activities may take very little money, but they all require time, and it's important to evaluate these investments in the same way.

If one of your marketing people is spending eight hours per week on social media, then allocate the time they are spending to each of the social media activities to make sure you understand the cost per click or cost per lead from these activities, just as you would from other paid media placements.

Once you have a good list of media options, it's important to make small bets with your limited marketing dollars on new media until you have a solid understanding of the cost per lead you can expect from each type of media.

I've seen marketing managers get very excited about a new type of Internet marketing program and allocate 75% of their budget to the media without any experience on how well it would perform. Making small bets is critical to testing. If you need to commit large dollars to one media just to buy in, it's very difficult to test it against other choices efficiently.

Creative Testing

There are a limitless number of creative options you can test in any given campaign. The concept, headline, graphics, photography, copy, and layout can all be tested.

When testing creative designs online, you can A/B test or multivariate test. A/B testing simply means that you position two fully designed creative options against each other. The critical part of this testing is that the creatives need to be seen by different parts of the same population at the same time in order for the test to be meaningful.

If you send the "A" email on Tuesday morning at 9 a.m. and the "B" email test on Saturday night at 10 p.m., you won't be sure if it was the time of week or the creative that determined the success of the design. If you show one website ad on the home page and another on an interior product page, the results won't be meaningful. If you run an ad on one keyword and the test on a different keyword, again, you won't get meaningful results.

You also need to make sure your test results are statistically significant. To do this, you'll need to do a little math to make sure you showed both ads enough times and that the results were different enough to tell you that one ad was the winner and the other was the loser.

Building the Plan

Once you have these elements in place, you are ready to develop the plan. The plan should start with a hypothesis that should give the rationale for the test, the test budget, how you plan to run the test, and the outcome you expect. In the hypothesis, I like to add a statement explaining the business impact so that you can start to make decisions about which tests you should run first, second, and so on.

Some tests are very expensive, and can be conducted quickly, and others need more time. For example, creating two competing TV ads might be a very expensive test, but might result in a strong ROI. Other tests can be run on less expensive media to learn something that can be used later on more expensive media.

In other words, you might run a test on your website to see which type of offer, an eBook or a white paper with the same title, is more effective. Based on this test, you can use the outcome to position the winner in an email campaign, a banner ad campaign, or a direct mail campaign, which is more expensive to run.

Record the Test Results

After you run a test, make sure that you document what you learn. A year or two in the future, a new team may be considering more options for testing and you want to make sure that they don't spend money to repeat a test you've already completed. If you are running tests on a regular basis for every campaign, you'll soon amass a steady list of results that will help you get better and better at producing consistent results.

Email Testing

Email is an important part of almost every online marketing program. Because of spam filters and because of how easy it is to opt out of email campaigns, it's important to make every email valuable and professional. You don't want to antagonize your users with miscellaneous testing emails that cause them to opt-out.

A key part of every email creative is the subject line. This is the headline for the email campaign that will either get the reader's attention or cause them to delete the email before they open it. Because of this, you should test the subject line first. The best way to measure the subject line is to evaluate the open rate. Even though it's not completely accurate, it's a good gauge for you to see if the subject line is doing its job.

Another important part of email testing is to evaluate the click-through rate. If the user opens the email, the click-through rate will tell you if the email itself is doing its job to get the user to take an action.

It's important to test both the open rate and the click-through rate to help you see if the email is effective.

Website Testing

Many organizations don't think about testing their own website, although this can be the most productive and lowest cost marketing vehicle to test. You should be tracking marketing results on your website with the same metrics you are using to evaluate other media. Impressions, clicks, and conversions can all be easily tracked.

Your website gives you the ability to rapidly create and deploy tests with no media costs. These tests can take the form of creative elements or ads on your homepage or other pages, and you can vary the design, offers, or messages on these ads, just as you do with other media.

Once you have your hypothesis and your ads developed, you can deploy them and get results on the click-through rate in order to see which message or creative is best.

The power of website ad testing is that you can learn quickly and then deploy these tested ads to other paid media.

Testing can drive a very high ROI for your marketing campaigns. If you use your imagination and then deploy the tests in a systematic and disciplined way, you can generate better results, build your confidence, and stay in the Zone.

Additional Resources

Visit www.marketing-in-the-zone.com for additional resources to help you develop your digital marketing plan.

- The **Zone Campaign Performance Reporting Matrix** will help you understand what to track in each campaign and give you a place to record weekly results for all of your marketing programs.

Get into the Zone
Leverage Resources
to Get Started

Creating a comprehensive digital marketing program that puts you in the Zone takes a big commitment in time and resources, but the payoff can be enormous. Not only will you deliver great marketing results, but you'll also become a more confident and secure marketer as you grow in your career.

I created www.marketing-in-the-zone.com to give you the tools and templates you need to get started so that you can take big steps in building your success and confidence. The first step in any improvement plan is to first understand you current situation, so take the **Zone Marketing Checkup** to get a good understanding of where you are today and identify your biggest challenges.

Next, you need to create a solid strategy so that you are focused on the right goals and the right target audience with the right message. To build the strategy you'll need to do your homework on your target market and competitors and create your core messaging. Use the **Zone Situation Analysis** to organize your research, and the **Zone Positioning** and **Segmentation Worksheet** to identify your best target markets. From there you can build a marketing plan and model using the **Zone Marketing Planning Template** for each campaign, which will forecast the results you plan to achieve with the budget you have.

Once you have the strategy in place, you can build the team you need to help you execute the plan. You'll want to find people that fit with your culture who can use all of the tools and techniques you outlined in your plan. You may build your team in-house or partner with an agency or service provider to get the right skills. Use the **Zone Marketing Team Assessment** and **Zone Service Provider Assessment** to make sure you have the right in-house people and service providers in place.

The next step is to make sure you have the right Marketing Technology Architecture in place to get everything done. Nothing in digital marketing happens without software, so you'll need to make sure you have the right software and you know how to use it. Use the **Zone Marketing Technology Assessment** to organize the information you gather about existing software, as well as evaluate new technologies.

With your strategy, plan, and team in place, it's time to start creating content. This might include website content, articles, infographics, video, or even long-form content like white papers. Content is the fuel that makes the marketing engine run, so don't skimp here or everything will be harder as you move forward. Use the **Zone Content Planning Tool** and **Zone Content Calendar** to create a strong and complete content plan.

The core of your marketing program will be your website, so take the time to do it right. All of your strategy, messaging and content comes together here and it will make all of your campaigns more effective if the design, architecture, and content supports your goals.

Once your website is ready, you'll be able to start your campaigns. You might use email, marketing automation, digital advertising, social media marketing, or search engine optimization to achieve your goals.

The **Zone Campaign Performance Reporting Matrix** will help you understand what to track in each campaign and give you a place to record weekly results for all of your marketing programs. These campaigns can be complex, so you'll want to bring your in-house team to Level 5, or engage experts who can help you use the best tools and the best processes to hit your numbers.

Marketing in the Zone is being confident that you have an integrated marketing program focused on the right audience with the right programs, and the right content at the right time. It's also about using data to make decisions and taking the guesswork out of where to spend time and money. When you do this well, you should experience less confusion and anxiety, and be confident of success.

The Digital Marketing Hack

ere's a quick list of things to work on so that you can make an immediate impact on your organization and take your first steps into the Zone. I've run through this checklist with hundreds of companies and have never found a company that was doing an excellent job in all areas. If you use this list to honestly assess your own digital marketing programs, I'm sure you'll find immediate opportunities for improvement. These items are the most common tactical issues I find with digital marketing campaigns, and you could double or triple your results within weeks, if you make these changes immediately.

1. **Website Home Page.** Look at your website home page. Do you have a call to action with a strong offer visible on the screen when you first arrive at your website? A call to action is something like, "download now," or "get a free consultation." If not, add the call to action now, and you'll see an immediate increase in traffic to your landing pages.

2. **Landing Pages.** Do your landing pages have a form visible on the screen when you first get to the landing page where people can give you their contact information? Do you give users a strong reason to give you their contact information? If not, write a strong call to action, and redesign your landing page immediately. This change will dramatically increase the number of leads or "conversions" you get from traffic to your landing pages.

3. **Digital Advertising.** Are your digital advertising campaigns taking visitors to well-designed, dedicated landing pages or to your home page? If you are paying to send traffic to your home page, you may be wasting money. By sending your ad traffic to good landing pages instead of your home page, you may double or triple your lead flow from advertising, and cut your cost/lead in half.

4. **Search Engine Optimization (SEO).** Use a tool like Spyfu to look at your organic search results compared to your competitors. Are you more or less visible than your competitors on important keywords? If you are behind your competitors, skip ahead to the chapter on SEO and implement better SEO tags on your most important website pages today.

5. **Email Lead Nurture.** If you are using a lead nurture email program such as HubSpot or Pardot, look at how many follow-up emails you are sending to each new lead. If you are only sending one, skip to the chapter on marketing automation, and create a simple email follow-up series to nurture new prospects.

6. **Social Media.** Look at the number of followers you have on each of the major social media networks compared to at least two of your competitors. Do you have more or less total followers? If you are behind, skip to the chapter on social media and start building your follower base as fast as possible.

7. **Analytics**. Look at the data you have available from tools like Google Analytics and any other marketing software you are using. Are you measuring your results? Do you have a simple dashboard that lets you track your progress? If you don't have integrated reporting software, open a spreadsheet right now and write down the number of visitors and leads per week for each of your campaigns. Very soon you'll start to see trends and be able to and make changes based on real data.

These quick hits are no substitute for an integrated digital marketing strategy and plan, but they will help you make an immediate impact in order to show results quickly. By taking action now, you'll be better equipped to go deeper once you fully understand the principles in this book and have a stronger plan in place.

About the Author

David Reske is a 20-year digital marketing veteran and author. He founded Onward Technology in 1994 and Nowspeed in 2003, and he has literally worked with hundreds of B2B and B2C clients in marketing strategy, search marketing (SEO and PPC), social media, email, marketing automation, and website design. David is focused on delivering world-class digital marketing services to clients across the U.S. through a team of awesome people. He is originally from Cleveland, Ohio and is a graduate of Ohio State University. David is also the former President of the Entrepreneurs Organization, Boston Chapter, and a regular host on Radio Entrepreneurs.

Morgan James
Speakers Group

We connect Morgan James published
authors with live and online events
and audiences whom will benefit
from their expertise.

Morgan James makes all of our titles available
through the Library for All Charity Organizations.

www.LibraryForAll.org

CPSIA information can be obtained
at www.ICGtesting.com
Printed in the USA
BVOW09s0924091017
497022BV00001B/3/P